Hertfordshire
COUNTY COUNCIL

Library Service

Please renew/return this item by the last date shown.

So that your telephone call is charged at local rate,
please call the numbers as set out below:

	From Area codes 01923 or 0208:	From the rest of Herts:
Renewals:	01923 471373	01438 737373
Enquiries:	01923 471333	01438 737333
Minicom:	01923 471599	01438 737599

L32b

- 5 DEC 1994	1 2 MAY 1997	- 7 JAN 2003
2 8 MAR 1995	2 8 FEB 1998	3 0 MAR 2004
1 5 JUN 1995	1 8 APR 1998	1 9 JAN 2007
	- 7 AUG 1998	
1 5 SEP 1995		2 8 OCT 2008
	1 0 JUN 1999	
1 2 JAN 1996	2 6 AUG 2000	
0 3 MAY 1997	3 1 MAY 2001	

L 33

The 1937-8 HORNBY BOOK of TRAINS

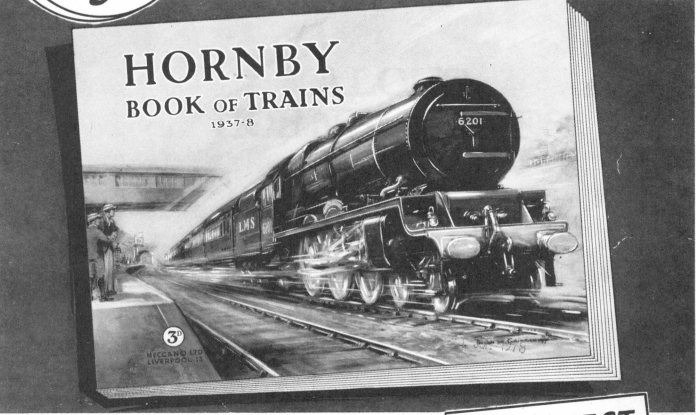

Of absorbing interest to Railway enthusiasts

The 1937-8 issue of the Hornby Book of Trains is the finest that has ever been produced. It contains splendid articles, fully illustrated by photographs, dealing with British express trains and locomotives, the mysteries of an engine shed, the fascination of operating a miniature railway, and other interesting topics.

In addition the book forms a complete catalogue of Hornby Trains for electric and clockwork railways. The Hornby Locomotives, Rolling Stock and Accessories are beautifully illustrated in full colour.

How to obtain the Book

The Hornby Book of Trains may be obtained from any Meccano dealer, price 3d., or direct from Meccano Ltd. (Dept. A.M.), Binns Road, Liverpool 13, price 4½d. post free. In the latter case a remittance in stamps should be sent and the name and address of the sender should be clearly written.

Readers living in Australia, New Zealand or South Africa who require copies should send their postal orders for 8d. (which includes postage) to the addresses given below. The Meccano Branch at Toronto will deal with Canadian orders and the price is 12 cents postpaid.

Readers living in countries other than those mentioned should order from Meccano Ltd., Binns Road, Liverpool 13, sending 6d. in stamps with their order.

Overseas Agencies:

AUSTRALIA: E. G. Page & Co., 52, Clarence St., Sydney (P.O. Box 1832k).
NEW ZEALAND: Models Limited, Paykel's Buildings, Anzac Avenue, Auckland C.1 (P.O. Box 129).
SOUTH AFRICA: Arthur E. Harris, 142, Market Street, Johannesburg (P.O. Box 1199).
CANADA. Meccano Ltd., 187-189, Church Street, Toronto.

Published by
MECCANO LTD. (Dept. A.M.), BINNS ROAD, LIVERPOOL 13

THE FINEST RAILWAY BOOK OF THE YEAR

GET YOUR COPY TO-DAY
Price 3D

FRANK HORNBY
15 May 1863 ~ 21 Sept 1936

ALONG HORNBY LINES

by

BERNARD HUNTINGTON

Oxford Publishing Co. · Oxford

SBN 0 902888 69 2

Acknowledgement

Permission to use the Trade Mark "Hornby" has been given by Rovex Ltd. who are the Registered Proprietors of the mark.

Line illustrations by Frank Burridge

Printed by B. H. Blackwell (Printing) Ltd. in the City of Oxford.

Photo reproduction and offset plates by Oxford Litho Plates Ltd. Oxford.

Published by:
Oxford Publishing Co.,
8 The Roundway,
Risinghurst, Oxford,
England.

HORNBY RAILWAYS

TIME TABLE

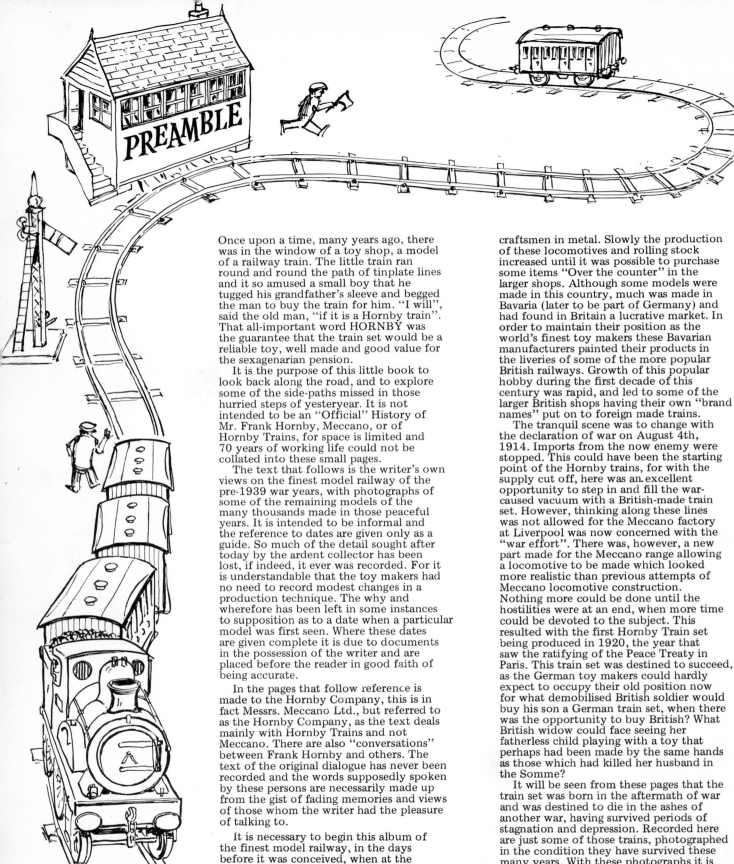

PREAMBLE

Once upon a time, many years ago, there was in the window of a toy shop, a model of a railway train. The little train ran round and round the path of tinplate lines and it so amused a small boy that he tugged his grandfather's sleeve and begged the man to buy the train for him. "I will", said the old man, "if it is a Hornby train". That all-important word HORNBY was the guarantee that the train set would be a reliable toy, well made and good value for the sexagenarian pension.

It is the purpose of this little book to look back along the road, and to explore some of the side-paths missed in those hurried steps of yesteryear. It is not intended to be an "Official" History of Mr. Frank Hornby, Meccano, or of Hornby Trains, for space is limited and 70 years of working life could not be collated into these small pages.

The text that follows is the writer's own views on the finest model railway of the pre-1939 war years, with photographs of some of the remaining models of the many thousands made in those peaceful years. It is intended to be informal and the reference to dates are given only as a guide. So much of the detail sought after today by the ardent collector has been lost, if indeed, it ever was recorded. For it is understandable that the toy makers had no need to record modest changes in a production technique. The why and wherefore has been left in some instances to supposition as to a date when a particular model was first seen. Where these dates are given complete it is due to documents in the possession of the writer and are placed before the reader in good faith of being accurate.

In the pages that follow reference is made to the Hornby Company, this is in fact Messrs. Meccano Ltd., but referred to as the Hornby Company, as the text deals mainly with Hornby Trains and not Meccano. There are also "conversations" between Frank Hornby and others. The text of the original dialogue has never been recorded and the words supposedly spoken by these persons are necessarily made up from the gist of fading memories and views of those whom the writer had the pleasure of talking to.

It is necessary to begin this album of the finest model railway, in the days before it was conceived, when at the beginning of this century a model railway if at all complete was the plaything for the children of the nobility and upper middle classes, people who had financial interests in the real railways of the day. Most of these toys were made to special order by craftsmen in metal. Slowly the production of these locomotives and rolling stock increased until it was possible to purchase some items "Over the counter" in the larger shops. Although some models were made in this country, much was made in Bavaria (later to be part of Germany) and had found in Britain a lucrative market. In order to maintain their position as the world's finest toy makers these Bavarian manufacturers painted their products in the liveries of some of the more popular British railways. Growth of this popular hobby during the first decade of this century was rapid, and led to some of the larger British shops having their own "brand names" put on to foreign made trains.

The tranquil scene was to change with the declaration of war on August 4th, 1914. Imports from the now enemy were stopped. This could have been the starting point of the Hornby trains, for with the supply cut off, here was an. excellent opportunity to step in and fill the war-caused vacuum with a British-made train set. However, thinking along these lines was not allowed for the Meccano factory at Liverpool was now concerned with the "war effort". There was, however, a new part made for the Meccano range allowing a locomotive to be made which looked more realistic than previous attempts of Meccano locomotive construction. Nothing more could be done until the hostilities were at an end, when more time could be devoted to the subject. This resulted with the first Hornby Train set being produced in 1920, the year that saw the ratifying of the Peace Treaty in Paris. This train set was destined to succeed, as the German toy makers could hardly expect to occupy their old position now for what demobilised British soldier would buy his son a German train set, when there was the opportunity to buy British? What British widow could face seeing her fatherless child playing with a toy that perhaps had been made by the same hands as those which had killed her husband in the Somme?

It will be seen from these pages that the train set was born in the aftermath of war and was destined to die in the ashes of another war, having survived periods of stagnation and depression. Recorded here are just some of those trains, photographed in the condition they have survived these many years. With these photographs it is the hope of the writer that the reader will be able to re-live and recapture some of the pleasures of those distant days when 6d. pocket money could be anticipated but not relied upon and a £1 note was a king's ransom.

The man who was to build the vast empire of Meccano, Hornby Trains and Dinky Toys, was born on May 15th, 1863 at 77 Copperas Hill, Liverpool. A district that was to be demolished between 1868 and 1871 to make way for the building of the new Lime Street Station. His father was John Hornby, a provisions dealer and Frank was one of seven children born to the Hornby family. Frank like so many boys of his generation was content to read books on adventure and engineering, for the world was full of such activities. He was a member of the Sunday religious teaching school known as the Band of Hope, and until 1887 little is thought to be of significance to the reader but in that year Frank married Miss Clara Walker Godefrey, a daughter of W. G. Godefrey. At this time he changed his employment and took the post of clerk with a meat import-ing company. The marriage was blessed with the birth of a son, Roland Godefrey in 1889, followed in 1891 with a second son, Douglas. Frank now had the task of bringing up his family on the modest wages he received for his position, a position which was to change as his employer realised the potential of their efficient clerk. His boyhood interest in engineering books had left its mark in the form of a yearning to make something and to this end Frank had a modest workshop in his garden shed.

In this environment the aspiring amateur strove with such problems as the solution of perpetual motion and on how to make his fortune. Many of his ideas did little for his fortune but did amuse his boys and his friends. One such friend was his employer David Hugh Elliott who was to encourage him further later on in years.

The family had gathered to celebrate Christmas one particular year when Uncle Frank produced his latest toy proclaiming it to be the fortune maker. The assembled family looked at the toy — it was a submarine — and decided that the obvious place to put it to the test was the bathroom. They ascended the stairs, the smaller feet reaching the bathroom first, just by way of a change. With the bath full of water all who could squeeze into the room saw the toy propel itself along the surface of the water, and at the pre-scribed time submerge and continue its course underwater. At the time to resurface something failed and the fortune maker sank ingloriously to the bottom of the bath, followed by an over-excited niece who fell fully clothed into the cold water.

Frank was also very interested in photography and was delighted when he was able to set his camera and quickly take his place in the family group before the shutter operated. Singing was another of his interests. He possessed a fine tenor voice and together with Clara, who is thought to have been a contralto, sang at charity concerts held in St. Judes Hall. He had now been promoted to Chief Clerk and had been working of late upon the idea of making a toy which could be dismantled without damage and reconstructed again in an entirely different form. The idea may well have been given to Frank by his brother whose employment as a stevedore brought him into closer contact with the mechanical world than that of the Chief Clerk.

Frank had been striving for some while to perfect the idea and said in his own words "the solution came to me whilst travelling in a railway carriage". At the earliest opportunity after the journey Frank was busy in his workshop being "aided" by his two sons. The task was to cut strips of metal of the same width to varying lengths, and at equidistances along the length holes were to be drilled. This took a considerable time and when the final pieces were shown to friends, his employer advised him to patent the idea before someone else did. The patent was duly issued on January 9th, 1901. Frank saw that he would have to find a manufacturer to make the parts if he was to continue with his Chief Clerks job. David Elliott, his employer and friend, realised the importance of the invention and gave Frank generous time off to scour the district and neighbouring counties for a manufacturer able to make the parts. Finally, one was found and with it came the realisation that the time had come to set up on his own, although money was short. The premises next to Elliott's office at 17 James Street were vacant and Elliott encouraged Frank to take them and form a partnership to be known as Elliott and Hornby, 18 James Street, Liverpool.

One evening Elliott introduced Frank to a Mr. Phillips who was impressed with the new "Mechanics Made Easy" toy and persuaded Frank to supply his Wholesale Company with the construction sets; this indeed was a good move for both men. Success was almost instantaneous, but unfortunately there were delays from the manufacturers resulting in parts not always being available to meet demands. The delays annoyed Frank, who saw the remedy in making the parts by Elliott and Hornby's own labour on their own machines. To enable this to become reality the partners decided to form a private company with a capital of £5,000 in £1 shares. The Company was to be known as Meccano Ltd., with a registered office at 12 Duke Street, Liverpool. The Company was registered in the Company's Register on June 4th, 1908 and seven persons subscribed the capital: Frank Hornby, Arthur Hooton, E. Warren, George Jones, M. Hill, L. Hill and O. Owen. Of these seven Hornby and Jones were to be directors together with Elliott. Production continued to grow and to outstrip the capacity of the factory once more.

A larger factory was found at 274 West Kirby Road, Liverpool, and the cost of financing the new premises was met by raising a £3,000 mortgage on the Duke Street premises.

So successful was the new Meccano previously known as "Mechanics Made Easy" that it was now eagerly sought by children and their parents, not only in this country but in the colonies and around the world, and yet again the factory was unable to meet the demands made upon it. There was at this time in the Old Swan area of Liverpool a large tract of waste land which had been reclaimed from some type of earthworks. The proposal was to develop the land with industrial building and Frank saw the opportunity to build a factory to meet his exact requirements. This was done and Meccano moved into Binns Road effectively on June 28th, 1914, not long before the tranquil society was thrown headlong into the war. Amid the tragedies of war Frank and Clara were to know their own personal tragedy, for on June 15th, 1919 their only daughter Patricia died in her 14th year. This great loss was always to be remembered by Frank and Clara, who benevolently endowed the nieces of the family in their activities and holidays.

Frank was never idle; his active brain was ever thoughtful of new ideas to expand and improve the Company. With Meccano safely launched on the road to success he turned his thoughts to the model train idea, shelved during hostility and with the full backing of the directors proceeded to develop the finest model railway yet seen. The Boardroom at Binns Road was a hive of activities and not as some thought a hide for the playing of bridge, a card game Frank particularly liked, frequently spending the evening in pleasant company playing the game. He also enjoyed dancing and was quite active upon the dance floor long after many of his contemporaries were coerced by age to "sit this one out".

With the country in a state of depression Frank crossed the rubicon by turning his Company into a Public Company with a capital of £300,000 made up from 200,000 Ordinary and 100,000 Preference shares. The directors were now to be Frank Hornby, George Jones, Hornby's two sons, Ernest Bearsley and Walter Hewitt, who was also the Company Secretary. There was now a London Office at 5/6 Marshall Street, but the main pulse was to remain at Liverpool where Frank was a much-liked and well-respected man. It was these qualities which prompted many of his friends to suggest to him that he should stand for Parliament in the 1931 General Election. Once the challenge had been given to him Frank strove to make every effort to win. He was adopted as the

Unionist candidate for the Everton constituency, a seat which had in the past few years changed its persuasions. In 1924, there was a Unionist majority of 630; in 1929 the electors returned a Labour majority of 1,567. Frank Hornby entered the three-cornered contest with all the vigour he had entered his previous undertakings and won the seat for the Unionists with 12,186 votes from Mr. Treleaven (Labour) 7,786 votes and the previous holder of the seat Mr. Hall-Caine 4,950 votes, giving Hornby a majority of 4,400 — a decisive victory for the local man. Upon entering the political arena Frank was necessarily away from the factory for much of the week whilst the House was sitting, coming back to Liverpool at the weekend, his chauffeur meeting the train at Lime Street Station and taking him direct to the factory. His arrival at the factory could be sensed by all, for the production seemed to go just that little bit faster for the last hours of Friday afternoon.

In these latter years of his life Frank's health had been failing slightly, diabetes had greatly affected his eyesight causing him a certain amount of difficulty in reading and he vacated the Chairmanship of the Board temporarily in favour of George Jones. Throughout his bouts of illness his devoted wife Clara was to be his constant nurse and companion. Having recovered from one such bout Frank noticed the effect the strain of his illness had upon his beloved Clara and had encouraged her to take a cruise, a fashion of holiday she had taken to in later years. Three young ladies made up the party — some were nieces — but all were of an age contemporary to that of Patricia. The party travelled to Southampton to board the Blue Star Line's finest cruise ship Arandora Star, which was sailing on September 5th, 1936 for the Mediterranean Sea. It was during this cruise that Frank's health deteriorated and it was necessary to admit him to The David Lewis Northern Hospital where after a short while his body gave up this life. The man who had given so much to the lives of others was now dead, but he was to live on wherever Meccano and Hornby Trains were to be seen. The news of Frank's death was published on the ship's notice board, but was not brought to the attention of Clara, for the ship was to be at sea for another seven days before arriving at Southampton on September 28th, 1936. It was a solemn elder son who boarded the 15,300 ton liner to break the news to the returning voyagers not only of the death of his father, but that the funeral had already taken place, to which many of the City dignitaries, the Directors of Meccano and many of his close friends attended.

Was the first model made by Hornby the Wagon or was it the Locomotive? A question of relative unimportance, and not answered here as this first section is devoted to the four-wheeled Goods Vehicles. The first type of wagon was the maid-of-all railway work, the Open Wagon referred to in these pages as type 1. The chassis was stamped out of mild steel, and pierced to accept the buffers, couplings, body and the axles. It was then folded to form a rigid base for the body. The body in the case of the Open Wagon consisted of two pieces, each bent to form one side and one end. These pieces were painted grey and in addition to the embossed planking, were pierced with a number of slots. Into these slots fitted tabs of metal letters representing initial letters of one of the great railway companies of the day. These side pieces were at an immediate disadvantage, as a separate pattern of slots were required for each railway company represented. This was soon realised by Hornby and a change to stencilled letters was made after about two years.

The whole wagon was assembled on the Meccano principle by nut and bolt, the couplings and buffers having threaded shanks to accept the Meccano nut. The wheels were kept in gauge by two split pins per axle and this type of wagon contained 33 separate pieces, excluding the initials *(see plate 1)*. Of the initials there could be up to four on each side, as the railway companies that Hornby chose at the beginning of the series were Great Northern; Midland Railway; London & North Western Railway; Caledonian Railway and London, Brighton & South Coast Railway, the latter being considered to be rare by some people these days.

This first type underwent changes before it was replaced by the type 2. Firstly, the brass coupling, which looked like something grandmother hung cups on the dresser with, changed to the more railway-like hook. This large nickel-plated hook caused the chassis to have a slot cut in the buffer beam to allow for the swivel action of the hook when negotiating a curved section of track. Some chassis came dual-fitted to take either type of coupling. As companion to the open wagon a box van was soon forthcoming, in which *plate 5* shows the Midland Railway version. Construction was similar to that of the Open Wagon, complete with "clip on" letters. With

opening doors the usefulness is apparent, for many a youthful owner carried live loads in the shape of white mice. Another change was the replacing of the clip on letters. It was soon realised that these letters were adding considerably to the cost of production and were hampering the chance of expanding the range of vehicles. A simple remedy was sought and found in the use of stencil-painted letters. The way was now open for development. By the painting of the basic van red and with the appropriate white stencilled letters the vehicle was now a Gunpowder Van, capturing the imagination of any boy. However, the door catch (*plate 10*) was a white metal casting, which could be broken by childish fingers or by impatient parents and this was soon changed for the brassed tin door catch. *Plate 9* shows one on the type 2 chassis Box Van.

From the introduction of the train sets and the additional rolling stock available the popularity grew until it was necessary to replace the much worn plant. The chance to redesign the basic chassis was taken and a more realistic railway-like chassis made. This is referred to here as the type 2 and was to be the standard for many years to come. The spring hangers were pierced to look more realistic and the brass buffers gave way to a malleable casting secured to the chassis by compressing the shank after being fitted through the hole in the buffer beam. The Meccano principle was slowly receding, but the body was still secured by four nuts and bolts. The wheels were now held in gauge by two niches pressed into the new thinner axle, and whilst still silver in colour had smaller centre holes to fit the smaller diameter axle.

As the popularity of these trains increased the range of models grew. A Milk Traffic Van complete with four milk churns and sliding doors on each side was introduced. Extra churns could be purchased in one of the accessories packets. The introduction of further types followed slight modifications to the type 2 chassis. The introduction of a new vehicle usually came in the autumn for the Christmas season, which was one of the best selling times. By Christmas 1925 there were 23 four-wheeled goods vehicles. One feature, that of mechanics, however simple, was a consideration of Hornby when designing a new model, as on the Crane Truck, on which the jib could be

CONTINUED ON PAGE 12.

2. *Believed to be one of the few still in captivity.*

1. *The component parts of the first type wagon totalled 33 pieces, excluding the initial letters.*

3. *A more detailed view of the early wagon.*

4. *Midland Railway Wagon showing all that remains of the early transfer.*

5. *A rather well used model of the early box van.*

6. *Great Northern Wagon with the first variation — the large hook couplings.*

7. *Inside the Open Wagon showing the method of fixing the initial letters.*

8. The first type of Van body painted red with white letters and mounted on the first type chassis.

9. The No. 1 Van, similar to the L.N.W.R. on the left, but now on the type 2 chassis and with 'brassed' door handle. Initial letters in gold with red shading.

10. Larger than life enlargement of the cast door fastener.

11. One of the many styles the No. 1 Van body was put to in the 1930's. The livery is pink with black chassis.

12. A lithographed Milk Traffic Van just for G.W. Enthusiast.

13. A similar lithographed body for the Fish Van, available in G.W., L.M.S. and N.E. liveries only.

14. *With duck egg green tilt, the Nord Wagon changed little over the years. Three flat wire hoops supported the cover; the ends being tied through an anchoring hole in each end panel.*

16. *Two pre-war companions, the Flat Truck with container. Each railway company container bore a different freight. The No.1 Lumber Wagon unlike the No.2 version came 'light'.*

15. *This post-war Milk Traffic Wagon is painted green whereas those of just pre-war were blue on a red base, and the louvres extended to the floor at all points. The first series of the Milk Traffic wagon were on type 2 chassis and painted grey/green livery.*

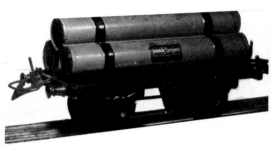

17. *This Gas Cylinder Wagon is from pre-war days, painted red and blue.*

slewed 360°, and the hook raised or lowered and kept in position by a simple ratchet. Another "mechanical" vehicle was the Hopper Wagon, the floor of which could be opened to discharge a load through the track into a receptacle below, *(plate 38).* The Snow Plough *(plate 30)* shows that it was to be pushed and was fitted with heavier wheels to offset possible derailments; the front axle having a pulley which, with the aid of a special rubber band, drove a shaft at right angles to the axle. The protruding end of the shaft was fitted to a fan, which when the vehicle moved rotated "expelling the snow" through an aperture in the surrounding cowling. A three-cylinder Gas Tank Wagon was a little unusual in this country, as most seen were of the one or two-cylinder variety. The prototype three-cylinder owed its origin to the Wagon Lits Co., who had them made to their own design for their Continental services. There was, however, a considerable influence of the Continental in the Hornby Series that the Gas Cylinder Wagon did not seem out of place. Other wagons of "Continental" appearance were a French type of Brake Van, and an Open Wagon with tarpaulin, now called a Covered Wagon. These wagons were lettered NORD, as was another Open Wagon that was fitted with the Brakeman's hut. Wine Wagons, a

double-barrelled one and a single-barrelled vehicle, were made helping to swell the "Foreign" influence, which was increased still further in 1931 with the introduction of a Barrel Wagon. The caption in the catalogue said the wagon was modelled on the type used in France, and this led the youthful mind to imagine that wine was the contents of his four barrels. The colour of the barrels changed from time to time and the final issue carried the label "CASTROL" OIL. Dashed were all hopes of the contents. As originally designed the four barrels were held in permanent place by two chains *(plate 27).* To tighten these chains there was a metal clamp between barrels 2 and 3, secured through a hole to the underside of the chassis. This pattern does not seem to have been very popular, for when the new type 3 chassis was introduced in 1932/33 the two chains were replaced by a single chain which was tensioned by a spring at one end. This gave the opportunity for the removal of the barrels and their refitting at the will of the operator. *Plate 26* shows another wagon with a Continental flavour — the Fibre Wagon — resembling a hamster's nest on wheels. The many empty chassis seen today can tell only that the bale of wood wool went one of the many ways to its destruction.

18. *Most of the Goods Wagons of this period (1925-6) carried their title on one side of the chassis.*

19. *Close-up of the first sliding door handle. This small piece needed to be bent, pushed through two small pierced holes and then fixed.*

20. *The version made during the 1930's, some painted in gay colours.*

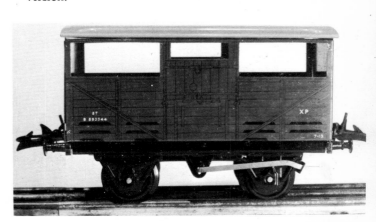

21. *A close-up of the latter pressed door handle which eliminated the costly operation of providing the former version.*

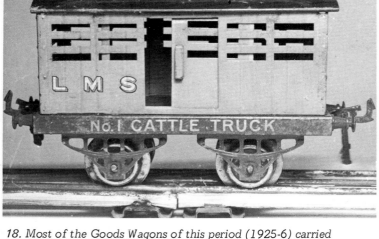

22. *The immediate post-war version in a more realistic livery of light brown.*

23. *Final version with lithographed body, handbrake lever and large open windows, through which the white mice 'cattle' of pre-war days would have escaped!*

24. The Single Barrel Wine Wagon on the type 2 chassis, painted red and green. The guerite giving a touch of French to a Liverpool made wagon.

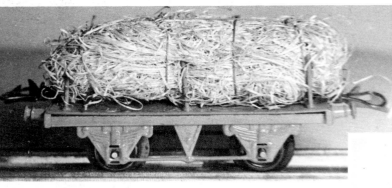

25. The Double Barrel version is of latter manufacture and uses the chassis of the older No. 1 coach.

26. The Hamsters Nest On Wheels is an apt name for this Fibre Wagon. The bundle of wood wool is held on to the base by six stanchions, generally blue, but this wagon is known in black and without the buffers; being the version supplied with the complete model railway sets.

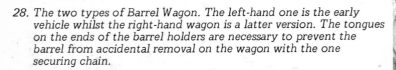

27. The Four Barrel Wagon in the first pattern with the two chains and clasp between barrels two and three. Vehicle painted red, and with barrels, painted blue, green and yellow at different times.

28. The two types of Barrel Wagon. The left-hand one is the early vehicle whilst the right-hand wagon is a latter version. The tongues on the ends of the barrel holders are necessary to prevent the barrel from accidental removal on the wagon with the one securing chain.

29. On the right is a closer view of the same vehicle.

30. The early type of Snow Plough, fitted with the special heavy wheels, sliding door and has a head light which is non-working. Painted in two shades of grey-green this one is unfortunate in that the roof and chassis have been repainted black.

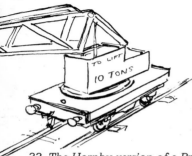

31. In yellow and blue livery and still fitted with the heavy wheels. However, the door does not open and gone are railway company initials.

32. The inside of the Snow Plough. The axle with pulley can be seen on the lower side of the floor; the cut-out section making the bearing block for the shaft protrude through the front end.

33. The Hornby version of a Breakdown Crane had an air of freelance about it. This Southern Railway one dates from around 1929. Earlier versions made in the 'nut and bolt' era had their title stencilled along the sole-bar.

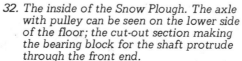

For the British-styled railways several more models were made, using the basic van body. Of these the Southern Railway seems to be least represented, as the Fish Van and the Meat Van were available for all Companies except S.R. A Railway Company Banana Van was available only in L.M.S., showing signs of local knowledge in the Design Department. Another Milk Traffic Van was forthcoming, but not so elaborate as the No. 1 Milk Traffic Van, as the sides were tin-printed with the louvres. Although the doors opened this was called No. 0 and was available only in G.W.R. livery. One van that would satisfy all the Railway Companies supporters was No. 0 Refrigerator with tin-printed body and non-opening doors. It was a good buy at 1/6d. in 1938. Another wagon was the open one in a blue livery, void of a number, but carrying the initials of the Great Four and fitted with a centre rail to support a tarpaulin, known as the wagon "B", presumably interpreted to mean "Bar". Most of these wagons had the chassis painted in anything but a railway-like colour — light green!

The majority of rolling stock once introduced, stayed as it seemed for ever. The Cattle Truck introduced on the type 2 chassis, remained a favourite and was last seen in post-war livery, similarly the No. 1 Luggage Van. One which was not re-instated was the Gunpowder Van; maybe those returning to their pre-war occupations had seen all they wanted with Gunpowder in the preceding five years. The No. 1 Milk Traffic, now slightly modified, came firstly in Southern livery, then as the "S" part of the British Railways and finally as "B", changing from green to red in the intervening years.

Reference is made in these pages that "Hornby" made this or that, or that the "Hornby Company" were responsible for some thing. This may give the reader the impression that Mr. Frank Hornby worked single-handed at all the tasks necessary in perfecting this wonderful model railway. Whilst he did much of the work in the early days of the Meccano production (as shown in the section on Frank Hornby), Frank Hornby had at the time of the introduction of the Hornby Trains a large factory covering nearly five acres of ground and employing well over 1,000 people. The Old Swan site was developed to his own design and the factory introduced many welfare facilities for the work force, which other manufacturers did not consider necessary to their workers' well-being. One such benefit was the canteen, where all who wished could purchase a hot midday meal at cost price, which for some was the only hot meal they could expect to consume that day.

Another feature installed by Hornby purely for the workers' benefit were large drying rooms, in which wet outer clothing could be dried whilst the owners were at their employment, the drying being effected by heated pipes in these rooms, which were locked during work time to guard against pilfering. Hornby paid well, on a par with other manufacturers of his day many thought, some thought less, but for their wages Hornby expected his people to work well and the discipline in the factory was very strict. No smoking was the rule, as it was in many other factories, but this rule was occasionally broken by Frank, who, finding it necessary to go into the factory, would invariably be puffing away at his favourite pipe, or in latter years at a cigar. This caused a little resentment on the factory floor, except in one department — the Tool Room. Here could be seen a haze of tobacco smoke over the machines caused by the men, who, having to work to the very fine limits set by the Company, aided their concentration with the occasional puff at their pipes or paused to roll a "gasper". No one said that they could smoke, but no one said they could not, despite the rules for good tool-room men were hard to find.

Hornby was proud of his factory, and justly so. He encouraged groups of people, particularly members of the Meccano Guild, to come and see how these fine toys were made. He personally escorted H.R.H. The Duke of York (later to be crowned King George VIth) on a tour of the factory in 1930, when he gave to the Duke a No. 2 special passenger train set as a present for his elder daughter. However, for the parties of visitors Hornby employed six smartly dressed young ladies to conduct them on the tour of the factory, causing them to make tactful excuses for the smoke in the tool room when questioned by chain-smoking visitors temporarily barred from their addiction. While mention of Mr. Hornby has taken preference over his products, another story is worth telling, if only to appreciate "the other side of the coin".

Returning home from the Great War, a young man, experienced and appalled at the art of war, pondered as to the best employment he could secure. His mother, fearing for her son's well-being, wrote and arranged an interview for employment with her brother. At the appointed hour the young man presented himself at the managing director's office at the Meccano factory. "Come in, Willie", said Uncle Frank. "It is very good of you to see me," said the young man from the other side of the glass-top desk. "So you would like a

job? Yes, I'll give you a job", and he rang the bell for the company secretary, instructing him to make the necessary arrangements.

The nephew was known to his family and friends as Bill or William and during the first week of his new job Bill was summoned to Mr. Hornby and was greeted with "How are you getting on, Willie?" The Willie pill was hard to swallow, but thinking of the job he had Bill swallowed hard and said "Fine, thank you, Uncle". "What are they paying you?", inquired Uncle Frank. "£3/10/-, Sir". "What?" Hornby's voice rose and he rang for the secretary. "Yes, Mr. Hornby, Sir", inquired the secretary upon entering the office. "Why are you only paying young Willie here £3/10/-?", asked the great man. "Well, Sir", replied the secretary, "£3/10/- is the going rate for a clerk", emphasising the word clerk. There was a very short pause then Mr. Hornby said, "I want him to have £5". The secretary replied saying that £3/10/- was already entered on his card. "Well, go and get his card and I will alter it". The episode ended with Bill getting a fiver a week, and a touch of animosity with the Company Secretary. This was one of several incidents which could have led to strained relations between Mr. Hornby, his relatives and the loyal company secretary, had it not been for the placid nature of the nephews, who now numbered three. The trio of nephews were putting in a full day's work in their respective positions, which in the views of some in high places was more than Frank's own sons should have been doing. For at times the two boys, like so many other boys, had not always seen eye to eye with their father. Now in the boardroom at Meccano headquarters.

A decision had been taken to start production of diecast models of people, trees, sheep and road vans, all for use as accessories to the railway. These were to be known as "Modelled Miniatures", as cumbersome name as "Mechanics made easy", so to find a more suitable name the company invited the executive staff to submit a list of ten names they thought to be suitable for the models and the directors would make the final choice. There is no record of the winner being given a prize. One of the names on the list submitted by Bill was a single word, used by his sister very often to describe something she thought was unique and fascinating as "DINKY". The name caught the imagination of all those present at the Board meeting and the name was adopted as Dinky Toys. Now boys were encouraged to start collecting Dinky Toys, which had a high degree of detail, were robust and had models of the latest cars available in the range. A range — which like those already introduced was to prove a winner.

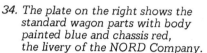

34. The plate on the right shows the standard wagon parts with body painted blue and chassis red, the livery of the NORD Company.

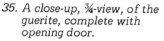

35. A close-up, ¾-view, of the guerite, complete with opening door.

36. Wagon 'B', in the usual rich blue livery on a black type 3 chassis, was supplied with a tarpaulin. The L.M.S. version is also known in 'serif' L M S. initials.

38. The Hopper Wagons were usually painted green with a black chassis. This one however, is red on a black type 3 chassis, modified to allow the doors to open at the bottom.

37. The No. 'O' Wagon in brown livery of the Southern Railway. When new it cost 1/3d.

39. The standard wagon in the post-war livery of brown and lettered L.M.S., it is interesting to note a new serial number and plastic wheels.

40. The post-war version of the well tried Hopper Wagon complete with B.R. number. The floor doors can be seen open in the centre of the wagon.

41. Although some of the American rolling stock was made in the U.S.A., this example of the 'American' Oil Tanker, was made in Liverpool.

42. The yellow livery of the Pennsylvania Box Car is highlighted by the black chassis, and with the opening doors the American 'Hobo' freighting it is not hard to imagine!

43. The American Caboose is known the world over thanks to the American Movie. Hornby's was also popular. Those that originated in the American factory had HORNBY LINES in place of the HORNBY SERIES in the lithograph design.

44. The American Pullman had a choice of two names "Washington" or "Madison".

45. Officially designated No. 'O', this small coach was the only other 'Mitropa' made. It had two types of lettering: Speisewagen (Dining-car) or Schlafwagen (Sleeping-car).

46. *An early Tilting Wagon, father of the Side Tipping Wagon. It is mounted on a modified type 2 chassis and comes from the days before the Civil Engineers' names were placed on the sides.*

47. *The No. 1 Rotary Tipping Wagon mounted on the type 2 chassis. The full flexibility can be seen. The wagon is painted in old gold.*

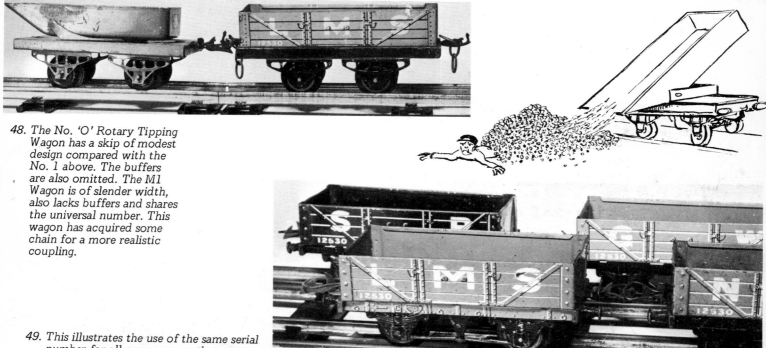

48. *The No. 'O' Rotary Tipping Wagon has a skip of modest design compared with the No. 1 above. The buffers are also omitted. The M1 Wagon is of slender width, also lacks buffers and shares the universal number. This wagon has acquired some chain for a more realistic coupling.*

49. *This illustrates the use of the same serial number for all open wagons that carry a number. All these wagons are the No. 'O' type, with the exception of the L.M.S. which is a No. 1 Wagon.*

50.

51.

52.

In making this review of the Hornby trains it is necessary to consider some of the other makers' interpretation of what was acceptable as a reasonable likeness to a prototype and yet competitive. All the wagons shown on this page, with the exception of one, were made by other "O" gauge model railway manufacturers and show by comparison that the Hornby version is the most austere. Having set up expensive plant making their models on the basic idea of Meccano — that they could be taken to pieces — it was several years before the design department produced the type 3 and *plate 49* shows the changes. Illustrating a lack of the imagination as they all bore the same number for many years, until the post war version as *plate 39* shows. The M.R. wagon (top left) came supplied with tarpaulin sheet and six sawdust-filled sacks. It was made by Bing of Nuremburg in 1910, but alas the price has been lost over the years. The adjacent L.N.W.R. came also from Nuremburg, this time from the Carette factory in 1912. These were the toys whose import into this country ceased with the death of a certain Archduke in 1914. How easy it is for the collector of today to "date" these vehicles of foreign make, as the date is incorporated in the lithograph. There is a chance that they were using up last year's stock. The small G.N. Wagon is also from Germany and was therefore made a little later (the others were from Bavaria), and is one that did get purchased in this country despite the aftermath of the war. The larger G.N. Wagon is of British manufacture by the Leeds Model Co. and uses wood covered with a paper lithograph for the body, the spring hangers and buffers being cast in white metal. Lastly the host on this page, the Hornby wagon of around 1922, shows the hook couplings, the embossed sides with clip-on letters, but lacking the detail given by the lithograph or tin-printing used on the other wagons.

53.

54.

55. Here is the first Refrigerator Van mounted on the type 2 chassis and carrying M.R. initials. Whether the other original Companies were represented in this model is now obscured.

56. Made by Bing for the British market, it has opening doors and a hand rail along each side. And has been 'improved' with chain couplings.

57. Bing made with automatic couplings of continental pattern and sliding door, also a British version with hook couplings.

58. The POOL Tanker shown in *plate 99* has a cousin here, assembled from parts not used up in 1940 before production was temporary halted. It was mounted on the type of chassis introduced at the recommencement after the war.

A Patent Idea

The need to patent an invention was very apparent to Frank Hornby; he had taken out his first patent for his invention now known as Meccano early in this century. Even with this precaution he had fought an action for infringement in the U.S.A. which it is estimated cost £70,000 before judgement had been granted in Hornby's favour. As a result of that action Hornby took out patents for many inventions and some now considered to be of a minor nature are listed here:

"Improvements in and relating to the track of toy railways", No. 253, 236 in 1925 was for the design of brackets to hold in place at the side of the track, the control wires of the Hornby Control System. *Plate 252* shows the bracket, and considerable patience was required to set up the system preferably for a permanent rather than portable layout. Patent No. 290, 121 was for the improvements in ball or roller bearings in 1928, and another Meccano invention for a "Dog Clutch" in 1929 carried No. 323, 234.

Improvements to toy steam engine units, also in 1929, shows yet another invention for the ever-popular Meccano. "Spring Driven Toy Locomotives", of 1931 No. 356, 567 enabled Hornby to fit a longer spring, giving a longer run per winding, thereby perhaps out-running a competitor's locomotive. Also for the Hornby Series was No. 366, 291 of 1932. This was concerned with the inner wrapping cardboard of the boxes in which the locomotives left the factory, perhaps normally made waste by the new owner, but not discarded by Hornby. With the aid of metal brackets the inner wrapping was formed to make a tunnel and looked fairly realistic with the cardboard printed to represent rock, verdure and the like. Keys came to the attention of Hornby for the Patent No. 368, 975 covered a more robust key than some previous versions, which may have left a tear-stained boy rather dissatisfied with his toy train set.

"Ramps for Toy Railway Tracks" No. 389, 188 of 1933 introduced a two-tongued plate, switchable to either tongue, to be fitted between the rails and when raised by means of a lever could stop or reverse the direction of a clockwork-driven locomotive. Until now a somewhat cruder metal tongue could be raised above the track to enable the locomotive to be stopped only. This method was not the same as those employed in the Hornby Control System.

Possibly the packing case tunnel sparked off the next Patent — that for "Interchangeable Rural Scenery" No. 397, 533 of 1933. This design was for cardboard units, of shapes that would fit the contours of the Hornby track, and in filling in the space between the closed loops of a track a complete landscape could be constructed, with trees and hedges fitting into special sockets on the base units. The units were printed as the tunnel; other rural scenes such as fields and cart-tracks were also available, and if used as intended the effect of the layout could be greatly improved. Whilst the idea was sound the cost was relatively high and probably deterred sales, for the scenery left the scene after only a short stay.

One Patent which was very important was No. 365, 701 "Improvements in Automatic Couplings for Railway Vehicles specially applicable to Toy Railways", and is worth investigating further. Up until now the accepted method of securing one vehicle to another was by a drop link hook coupling, and this hook or slight variations were used by most of the toy train makers. Now Hornby had the opportunity to introduce a fully automatic coupling. The chance was too great to lose and he instructed Messrs. A. J. Davis, his Patents Agent, to draw up the necessary documents, submitting them dated November 17, 1930 on the following day. This provisional specification contained some 800 words and outlined the use and the design. To this the British Patent Office allocated No. 34652/30 and

production of the coupling could now proceed without fear of rivals making an early copy of the auto coupling. June 10, 1931 saw the depositing of the complete specification which went into great details with drawings as to the need to shape the wire loop in the fashion now so familiar. Included also is the wire connection between the coupling and the bogey trucks — explanation being given that there was a need to keep the two adjacent couplings in the line with the centre of the track if successful coupling was to be achieved on a curved section of track. This Patent specification was finally accepted on January 28, 1932.

Plates 59—62 show the imprinted numbers on the couplings; shown also are some other numbers of significant interest and illustrate the degree of protection sought by Hornby to cover the automatic coupling. The small + preceding No. 157977 is not a symbol of addition, but the symbol of Switzerland. In that country application was made on June 26, 1931 and fully accepted on October 31, 1931, being given retrospective priority to November 18, 1930, the date of the British provisional application. This was granted under class 54F of the Swiss Patents Acts by the Bureau Federal de la Propriete Interectuelle. Patents were also sought and granted in France and Belgium, but these were safeguards to prevent agencies from acting in favour of the other great toy-making country, Germany. To protect his invention in that country Hornby applied to the German Patents Office on June 23, 1931 seeking again retrospective priority to November 18, 1930, and this was granted under section 77F of the German Patents (Utilities) Acts and was given No. 1179362. To identify this as being granted in Germany the letters D.R.G.M. were also imprinted into the coupling. These letters do not bear any resemblance to the tag pre-war boys attached to their meaning, but stand for "Deutsches Reichs Gebrauchs Munster"; it also does not signify that the articles were made in Germany.

59.

60.

61.

62.

The German Utilities registration was granted for a period of 3 years, with the option of renewing for a further 3 years which was the maximum available, providing the fee for renewing the Patent was forthcoming. The Fees payable in this country in connection with the automatic coupling were £1 when the first application was made and a further £4 when finally accepted. This gave cover for a total of 5 years from the date of the original application. The renewal fee for subsequent years increased by £1 per year, year 6 costing £6, and this could continue until year 16 was reached when the fee would be £16. In addition year 16 would be the last year such a patent could be renewed. However, before this period could elapse the directors of Meccano reviewed, or failed to review, the situation in 1937 and the renewal fee was not paid, causing the Patent No. 365, 701 to lapse at the end of the 7th year.

63.

Continuing in retrospect the review of 4-wheeled stock, consideration is now given to Brake Vans and 4-wheeled Passenger stock. Firstly, the Brake Vans. Shortly after the first train set was seen to be running "open ended" Hornby produced on the type 1 chassis a brake van styled after the massive 8 wheelers with the double verandah seen on the Great Northern Railway. The Hornby version had 4 wheels as *plate 64* shows. At about the same time another van was also produced, again styled after an 8 wheeler on the L.N.W.R. with one verandah. These two designs were accepted as the patterns for many years to come, changing chassis and liveries as the time passed. However, vans do not appear to have been painted in the liveries of the other three companies of the original five railway companies. The G.N. became L.N.E.R. and the L.N.W.R. became the L.M.S., as did their respective prototypes. After a few years the L.M.S. pattern van doubled as the Goods Brake for the G.W.R. and looked remarkably like the heavy vans seen in the great yards of Acton or Builth Wells. Some six or seven years after the first van appeared it was decided to make a van for the Southern Railway, and by use of the L.N.E.R. pattern painted in chocolate brown and lettered S.R. in white all four main line railways were catered for. As the type 3 chassis became available it was fitted to the brake vans, and their production was to continue until 1940. Some were fortunate to make a brief re-appearance in post-war days – these being the L.M.S. and L.N.E.R. – and now fitted with lamp irons at each end of the van as in real practice. This was a short period in their life span, for with the Nationalisation of the railways in 1948, the L.N.E.R. lettering was replaced by "E" and that of the L.M.S. to "M". This was only the herald of a period of all change as the now old, but well tried, type 3 chassis was nearing the end of the line, being replaced by a semi-diecast base upon which was placed a lithographed body representing the Midland Region of British Railways.

The price of this type of vehicle was 4/- in 1925, and down to 3/6d. during the years of the depression. 1935 saw the price reduced even lower to 2/11d., and four years later to 2/9d. Whilst mentioning costs, voices could be heard in the main office corridor one afternoon coming via the open door of a costing clerk's office. It caused the area to be quickly evacuated for fear it might just as suddenly turn on you and demand what you were doing.

Through the open door could be heard a voice, thought to be that of Mr. Hornby questioning a clerk of many years standing as to what is gain? "Well, Sir" explained the humble clerk, "the costs are Material Xd., Labour Xd., Finishing Xd., Advertising Xd., Administration Xd., Retailers profit Xd., giving a gain of X". Before the clerk could finish his explanation of the cost breakdown Mr. Hornby was heard to say "GAIN? What do you mean gain?" "Well, Sir, gain is gain —". "Do you mean profit?" said his employer. "Er, yes Sir, gain or profit Xd." The matter settled the air returned to its accustomed calm and tranquillity.

The method of supplying retailers in the United Kingdom was for one of the Company's four salesmen, each supplied with a motor car, to visit the retailer. There was usually one retailer per town, the larger towns perhaps having two or more. The salesmen would take the order and supply publicity material. All goods ordered would be sent direct from the factory, and in this fashion the retailers profit could be a little larger than if a wholesaler was used. It was, however, insufficient for one particular retailer who had a chain of shops across the country. This company endeavoured to negotiate a further 1% but to no avail with the Hornby Company, a profit of 33% only available to any retailer. In consequence the chain store sold up their stock of Hornby trains and the other Meccano products.

Returning to the trains the 4 wheeled passenger stock introduced by Hornby had a vague resemblance to some of the then main line companies' saloon or open coaches. The roofs were rather flat and the windows were cut-out, and as a line they were rather short-lived. Despite that there are many still in existence in the hands of devotees of the Hornby Series. The next coach was available in L.N.E.R. or L.M.S. liveries, having opening doors and clerestory roofs. There was also a full brake version, both patterns being mounted on a chassis similar to the type 2 goods chassis but a little narrower. They were supplied in train sets but could be bought separately for 3/6d. (1925). Modernisation removed the clerestory and increased the range to include G.W.R. and S.R. Now known as the No. 1 Passenger Coach they continued until the automatic coupling arrived when more changes took place giving the Coach and the Guards Van a new chassis fitted with the auto-coupling, slightly wider body with semi-elliptical

roof and "battery boxes" beneath the sole-bar, but gone were the opening doors. These vehicles were the mainstay of many small layouts, and continued in production until the war. As with other vehicles which re-appeared after the war only the L.N.E.R. and L.M.S. patterns were made, being a little different in the colour of the livery than their pre-war cousins. When the British Railway livery of red and cream started to appear on main line stock the Hornby coaches changed too and a new pattern in the style of the main line corridor stock was made on four wheels.

Luxury trains were popular with Hornby as can be reflected in the number of such coaches that were available in the Hornby Series, in the humblest range, the M.O. the only passenger coach was a Pullman with a choice of two names, Joan and Zena. Some of the first Hornby Pullmans (cost 1/-) were void of buffers and were known as M.2. This pattern changed little but later versions had a choice of three names. At the top of the four-wheeled Pullmans, the No. 1 range, had opening doors, cut-out windows, and a choice of three different names. All this could be bought for 3/6d. each; a companion brake cost 6d. more and had but one name.

Also in the four-wheeled coach range were an American Pullman, with a choice of two names — "Washington" or "Madison". The same coach pattern as the "American" type, but in the livery of the German Mitropa was also available. This, too, was available in two types of lettering as the large bogie version, one for the Dining Coach and one for the Sleeping Coach. Whilst with the four-wheeled coaches, mention of a special little train should be made. It was at the time of His Majesty's Silver Jubilee that the L.N.E.R. Company designed a special streamlined locomotive and matching train calling the locomotive "Silver Link". The whole showpiece ran over the L.N.E.R. mainline and was admired by all, and there were opportunities for special visits by schoolchildren to depots where the great train was open for inspection. There were also opportunities for Hornby, ever abreast of the times, to introduce a model of the train, not a large expensive model that would be only for the wealthy, but a simple cheap train set for the young (and sought now by the not so young). The little locomotive in the M.O. range fitted with a new streamline body and stylish tender was to haul the special articulated

CONTINUED ON PAGE 26

24

64. The first of a long line of Brake Vans dating from 1922.

65. The two pre-war versions of the single Verandah Brake Van.

65a. Insert photo of makers transfer from the late 1920's.

67. This 'just pre-war' S.R. Brake Van is mounted on a green chassis.

66. An early L.N.E.R. Brake Van brown livery and silver wheels.

68. Post-war version of the double verandah now lettered N.E. and fitted with three lamp irons, needing a special red painted lamp for the side mounted irons.

coach, tin-printed to represent the new coaches of the prototype, and mounted on a special six-wheeled chassis pivoted in the centre simulating the articulated feature of the main line stock. Although the unit was attractively up to date, the popularity soon fell off and in order to use the large number of parts already made the Silver Jubilee train set remained available, but there was the same set now painted in two tones of green or in a maroon and cream livery, similar to that which was to adorn the prototype so many years later.

Since the first train set there had been an addition to the standard range a similar but slightly cheaper version of most of the items, whether locomotive, wagon, station or signal. A slight change in the design such as omitting the buffers could save both the cost of providing and fitting them. These costs fractional as they were enabled Hornby to sell to a wider public. Hornby labelled the ranges or series as "O", "M", No. 1, the true meaning of the "O" and "M" can now only be left to the past, the No. 1 and the No. 2 series refer to the four and eight wheeled versions of similar vehicles. Hornby introduced a new range intended for the very young, the M.O. range. The whole design of the range was petite by comparison, but ran on the "O" gauge track. There was also a range of track made for the M.O. series, consisting of 9" radius curves and a similar radius point of a simple turn-out pattern. To allow the train to be used by the very young a new coupling was made in the form of a peg or tab and a "D"-shaped hole. The whole of this range could not be successfully coupled to the other series. There were available in the M.O. range an open wagon, petrol tanker, crane truck, with simple working crane, a side-tipping wagon, rotary tipping wagon, and for the "passengers" the Pullman Coach mentioned earlier and the Silver Jubilee or streamlined coaches.

69. The new and the old! The type 20 Passenger Coach on the left was a post-war adaption of the pre-war Pullman in the M.O. range.

70. The first type of 'M' Pullman.

71. Post-war version showing that little has changed in the intervening 30 years.

72. The No. 1 Pullman. These earlier vehicles had opening doors, and all had names — a choice for the parlour car but just one for the composite.

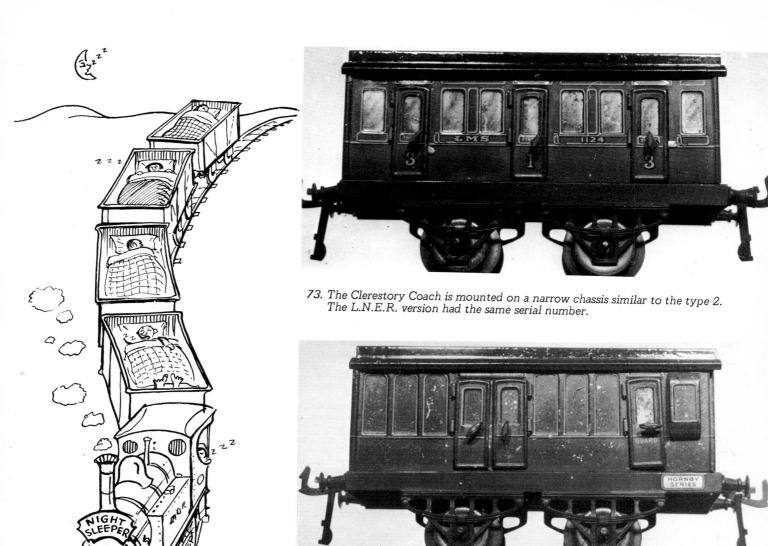

73. The Clerestory Coach is mounted on a narrow chassis similar to the type 2. The L.N.E.R. version had the same serial number.

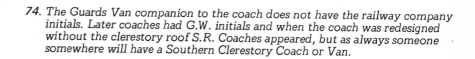

74. The Guards Van companion to the coach does not have the railway company initials. Later coaches had G.W. initials and when the coach was redesigned without the clerestory roof S.R. Coaches appeared, but as always someone somewhere will have a Southern Clerestory Coach or Van.

75. The later No. 1 Passenger Brake Van of post-war days, very similar to the pre-war version.

76. British Railways livery on a well tried coach.

Some of the more colourful wagons in the Hornby Series owe their liveries to being "Replicas" of vehicles owned by nationally known companies and run privately on the mainlines. The policy appears to have been that the Hornby Co. would select a few well known companies, making anything from Petrol to Chocolate and propose that Hornby would produce a toy railway vehicle carrying the name of their company and trade-marks, if the Company would pay the costs of the transfers. Most of the companies approached were only too ready to co-operate in this way, for they were aware of the immense power this medium of advertising had. For by this method their name was being displayed in many more shop windows than possibly the products were sold in, it also brought their name into people's homes, long before the modern intrusion of the television commercial. Some schemes were short lived, either due to the advertiser not wishing to pay for a further batch of transfers, or by the Hornby Co. removing the wagon from the range, as perhaps it did not sell well. Many of the companies that took part in the scheme are still expanding production, but few recall the part they played in the production of these Private Owner wagons. Possibly the first of these was the Shell Petrol Tank, made on the type 1 chassis and when the type 2 chassis became available additional liveries were produced, and by 1925 there were three tanks "National Benzole"; "Pratts"; and of course "Shell", all priced then at 3/-. Many of the European makers of tank wagons gave a vehicle with an opening "filler", which over the years could have been lost, or worse, allowed fluids to be placed inside the tank, which was not in the least bit water tight.

Tank wagons proved to be popular, and by 1939 there were eight including one in the M.O. range and another styled after the pattern of the American Tank Car. The words "Super Tanker" are nowadays associated with the giants of the seas, but had the phrase been coined in the 1930's it could have been used to describe another tank wagon. This was not called a No. 2 as it was still on a four-wheeled chassis, but there the resemblance with the other tanks stopped. The body was larger in diameter, a ladder gave access to a more realistic filler cap, but still non-opening. Attached to the chassis were two bolsters, tensioned against the tank by two tie bars each side, anchored to the centre of

the chassis side. This splendid wagon bore a resemblance to the six wheeled tanker wagons seen for many years on the G.W.R. The 1930 version on the type 2 chassis carried the United Dairies decal, and the 1939 wagon now on the type 3 chassis carried "Nestles Milk". Using the same vehicle with a change of paint and livery and minus the ladder Hornby produced a wagon labelled "Colas", this being the Trade name of a Company manufacturing Bitumen. Colas came in around 1930 and was 6d. cheaper at 5/- than the United Dairies Tank Wagon.

Of the Box Vans in the Private Owner range the livery of the first depicted a bulls head, a splendid transfer and pertaining to the Colmans Mustard Co. This van was a short lived vehicle, although some are still known to exist. Seccotine, which appeared possibly at the exit of the Colmans Van, was blue with an orange roof and was to stay from 1925 up until the war. Three large biscuit makers, Messres. Carrs, Crawfords and Jacobs, all had vans, which lasted as the Seccotine van did. Messrs. Crawfords having a factory next to the Meccano factory in Binns Road. Messrs. Cadbury's Van came with a blue body and gold lettering and was seen around 1932, and a year or so earlier a yellow van with the motif of Fyffes Banana Co. on the door reminded us to ask mother to buy some bananas. A late comer to the box van Private Owners range was Messrs. Palethorpe, makers of Royal Cambridge Sausages. Moving to other fields Civil Engineers' names were appearing on the sides of the Rotary Tipping Wagon and the Side Tipping Wagon. The Cement Wagon which was originally painted grey and later red, carried railway company initials, changed its coat to yellow and took the name Portland Cement. Naturally, Meccano and the Hornby Railway Company had their names on Open Wagons, but none of the Coal Merchants whose names were emblazoned on the real coal wagons of the day were featured. Before the restrictions of the Government's wartime regulations caused the production of toys to be seriously curtailed, the Meccano factory took the opportunity to keep up to date and produced a Petrol Tanker in "Wartime" livery. All petrol resources had been pooled under Government policy and Hornby produced a drab grey painted tanker with **POOL** painted in white letters in August 1940 at a cost of 1/11d. (*Plate 99*).

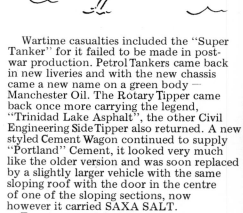

Wartime casualties included the "Super Tanker" for it failed to be made in post-war production. Petrol Tankers came back in new liveries and with the new chassis came a new name on a green body — Manchester Oil. The Rotary Tipper came back once more carrying the legend, "Trinidad Lake Asphalt", the other Civil Engineering Side Tipper also returned. A new styled Cement Wagon continued to supply "Portland" Cement, it looked very much like the older version and was soon replaced by a slightly larger vehicle with the same sloping roof with the door in the centre of one of the sloping sections, now however it carried SAXA SALT.

Eager eyes watched the toyshop windows for signs that other pre-war favourties would return, instead eyes had to become accustomed to the smaller Hornby Dublo, which born just before the war was now being weaned on the metal ration that was available. With the advancements made in the post-war years in the field of plastic moulding there was a faint hope that this material could be used to replace metal, but all that was made in plastic were wheels for the 'O' Gauge trains.

77. The first type of Petrol Tanker mounted on the first type chassis with hook couplings and 'silver' wheels. The dummy filler on top of the tank has a familiarity to the safety valve of the No. 2 engine with slight modification.

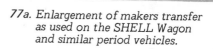

77a. Enlargement of makers transfer as used on the SHELL Wagon and similar period vehicles.

78. UNITED DAIRIES not in the same condition as in *plate 80* but it is just a few years older.

79. This early blue body COLAS Tanker has lost the tie-rods.

80. The NESTLE version on the type 3 chassis showing details of the 'super tanker' on blue painted chassis.

81. ROYAL DAYLIGHT in pre-war days.

82. REDLINE on type 3 chassis, but with hook couplings. Not rare but from the time of the early 1930's using up parts before the automatic coupling became universally fitted.

83. With an attractive blue body and orange roof. Later versions had automatic couplings, sliding doors and was fitted to the type 3 base.

84. CARR'S Biscuit Van was blue, and that of JACOB'S was finished in crimson lake and that of CRAWFORD'S in red.

85. With yellow body, red roof, red or black chassis and blue and white motif.

86. Blue body with gold letters is the livery for CADBURY'S CHOCOLATES.

87. Side Tipping Wagon shows how the tip was simply effected. The post-war version was very similar.

88. The last of the Private Owner Box Vans made just before the war, this one has inherited a set of plastic wheels.

89. COLAS Tanker has red tank and is the later version. On this model the Hornby transfer is on the tank end.

90. Another wagon from the period when the type 3 chassis was fitted with the small hook couplings. The B.P. livery on this wagon was similar to that used for the M.O. Petrol Tanker.

91. CEMENT in gold letters on a red body, for this wagon the roof door is open. Earlier versions were in the grey livery, latter models in yellow.

92. New livery for the post-war, apex roof vehicle slightly larger than the Cement Wagon made after the war, but still with the opening roof.

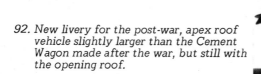

93. Post-war version of the Rotary Tipping Wagon.

94. The Coal Wagon in red livery gold shaded 'Meccano' fitted with embossed coal. A similar wagon lettered 'Hornby Railway Co.' was also available.

96. The MOBILOIL on a type 3 chassis and painted grey with white motif.

95. A rather paint-scratched PRATTS Tanker on the type 2 chassis.

97. SHELL Tanker on the type 3 chassis.

98. A slight change. The CASTROL tank has the later type of 'filler cap', a dark green livery and gilt lettering.

99. The wartime POOL Petrol in light grey, and costing 1/11d when introduced in 1940.

100. The post-war version in light green for the MANCHESTER and yellow for the SHELL.

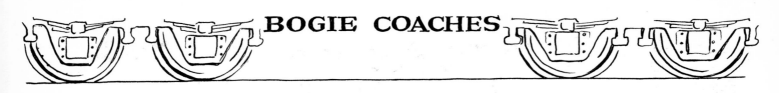

Bogie Rolling Stock first appeared in the "Nut and Bolt" era, with a Pullman Coach in a green and cream livery. A second coach in similar colours but lettered "Dining Saloon" carried the Coat of Arms of the Railway Company that it pertained to represent, the same five favoured companies that could be found on the first open wagons.

The introduction of the Electric (H.V.) Metropolitan Train brought a new coach, the first by a new-to-Hornby technique, that of lithography. Hitherto the coaches were enamelled. Parts of the "Met" were still enamelled, but the sides carried a good copy of the coaches seen working out of Baker Street. Two were made, namely a full 1st and a 3rd Brake, and as these coaches were to be hauled by an electric powered locomotive it was possible to have them lit. This was done by the use of small flexible leads fitted to the ends of the coaches and connected to the locomotive. The H.V. (high voltage or house voltage) system was abandoned after only a short while, due mainly to an apparently lethal potential presented to the operator who might endeavour to re-rail the locomotive without first switching off the supply. The coach was redesigned for the low volt system and used a roller pick-up on each of the two bogies for collecting the power for the lights, there was also a switch for "daylight" working.

By 1928 the Pullman had been given a new body, which could still be taken apart and re-assembled if required. Gone was the green and cream livery, being replaced when the actual Pullman Car Company changed to chocolate and cream with a similar pattern. Now the doors were able to be opened and the windows glazed with a celluloid sheet with printed Pullman table lamps. This Pullman, known as the No. 2 Pullman, was to remain in production until that unhappy day in 1939 which caused production to cease in due course.

Using the same type of body, and with a maroon coat of paint and lettered L.M.S. Hornby introduced a Saloon Coach much after the style of that Company's "Club Coach". Similarly the same body with a brown livery and lettered L.N.E.R. made a Saloon Coach. Unhappily neither the G.W.R. nor the Southern were represented in this type of coach.

Time was ripe to introduce yet another Pullman, which was to be superior to the No. 2, called at first the 2/3 Pullman, later changed to the title No. 2 Special Pullman. These were grand indeed for the coach had in addition to the normal features on the No. 2, roof ventilators, an ornate livery, names as the prototypes, and equalising bogies. These coaches were in the style of the Parlour Car, and the Composite Brake Coach, this had in addition to the opening doors, double luggage doors in the composite section.

Returning to the mid 1920's, the Wagon-Lits Company had built in this country, for use on the new Calais—Mediterannee Express a complete train made up of Dining Saloons, Sleeping Coaches and of course Luggage Vans. Hornby was soon to follow, producing a French type locomotive (more of this in another section) and a Dining Car followed in a short while by a Sleeping Car, all in the blue livery of the Wagon-Lits Company and with gilt lettering along the cant-rail exclaiming to all, COMPAGNIE INTERNATIONALE DES WAGON-LITS ET DES GRAND EXPRESS EUROPEENS. What an opportunity for the schoolboy learning French to be able to recite that phrase when asked "to say something in French", for the benefit of the wealthy, much travelled aunt visiting for the afternoon. With such a show of expertise her departing gesture may well have provided the necessary funds, 14/- (1930) for the purchase of one of these luxury coaches. Hot on the trail of Wagon-Lits came their European rival Mitropa, this Company supplied similar services to the travelling public in Germany for the State Railways. For their model of the Mitropa Coaches Hornby, the same coach structure as the Riviera Blue, painting it in red with gilt lettering as were the prototypes. Two types of lettering were available, again a Dining Car and a Sleeping Car. These Mitropa coaches did not appear in the Train Sets as the Riviera coaches did and from the small numbers seen today production from 1931 until 1940 must have been on a very limited scale.

Little had changed for some years in the bogie carriage sheds, and the obvious lack of coaches representing the four Mainlines was beginning to be noticed. When eventually production of suitable coaches began all four main companies were represented, with the express trains having true to type features and corridor connections. Known as the No. 2 Corridor Coach it was available as a first/third and a brake-composite. The Southern variety being an open third instead of the first/third. These corridor coaches were very satisfactory for the express trains and in 1935 eight more bogie coaches were introduced for the local trains, two each for the four companies, and titled No. 2 Passenger Coach. They measured 11¾" over the buffers as the Corridor type did, but were 6d. cheaper at 7/- in 1939.

Of all these coaches available before the War, only the No. 2 Passenger Coach was to be made when production began again. The colour of the roof was different from its pre-war cousin and production was very limited as metal was now in short supply. With the increase in popularity of the "OO" scale, consideration was given to the fact that one No. 2 Passenger Coach used the same amount of tinplate as several "OO" coaches, and as stocks of parts were exhausted this slender stream ceased.

101. The first Pullman, shown on the left is fitted with brass buffers, cut-out windows, but with non-opening doors.

102. Resplendent in dark blue with gold lettering, the companion coach was the Dining Car.

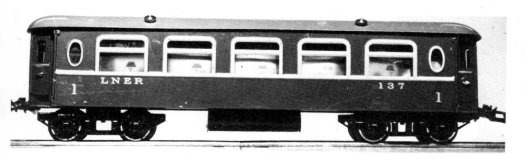

103. The No. 2 Saloon Coach in a brown livery which bore little resemblance to the teak livery of the L.N.E.R. The L.M.S. version is painted in maroon. The table lamps are stencilled on to the window glazing.

104. The first series of No. 2 Special Pullmans had cream painted roofs. Nine names were used for these: PHOEBE, VERONA, MONTANA, ZENOBIA, LORAINE, IOLANTHE, GROSVENOR, ALBERTA and ARCADIA.

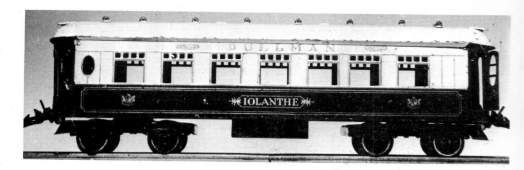

105. The No. 3 MITROPA Coach, painted red with gilt lettering. The companion coach is lettered SCHLAFWAGEN.

106. Here is the companion coach. It was a great pity that there was not a German State Railway locomotive produced to haul these vehicles.

107. Here for comparison is a coach made for Bassett-Lowke by a Foreign Manufacturer, possibly German, for the British market. This model has inherited a set of scale bogies.

108. The No. 2 Special Pullman ARCADIA in the livery of the middle series.

109. The Bogie photograph on the right shows the pivot hole between the spring hangers which effected an independent suspension action on the four wheels.

110. The picture on the left shows VERONA from the final series in the few years before the war.

111. Corridor connection in place between two L.M.S. Coaches.

112.

The tin printing process gave a good appearance of the L.N.E.R. Teak Coaches. The design of the L.M.S. main line coaches was faithfully copied in those shown below, including the mounting of the destination boards on the side of the coach.

113.

114.

115.

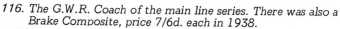

116. The G.W.R. Coach of the main line series. There was also a Brake Composite, price 7/6d. each in 1938.

116a. No.2 G.W.R. Suburban Coach.

117. Composite side of the contemporary Southern Railway Coach.

117a. No.2 L.N.E.R. Suburban Coach. There is of course a 3rd class Brake version.

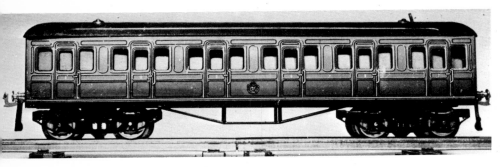

118. The 1st class version of the Metropolitan Coach. The sides and ends are held to the chassis by the nut and bolt method. The roof is secured by four milled edge screws similar to battery terminals: Cut-out windows glazed with yellow celluloid. Although the doors were non-opening, the detail, including the 'MET' coat of arms, is quite remarkable.

119. Shown on the right is the standard bogie with the additional platform carrying the roller pick-up insulated from the bogie by a 'paxolin' type of board. The electric lead can be seen protected by the use of an eyelet where it passes through the chassis. Both bogies were of the same design with brass buffers secured by Meccano nuts. The bright silver wheels were mounted on a thin axle.

120. On the left can be seen the inside of the coach. The internal lights are mounted on the roof support, one at each end, but only one of the two had the switch for turning off the light for daylight running. The sheet of celluloid can be seen bending with age.

121. The 3rd class Brake version was very similar. The light switch can be seen to the right of the roof bolts. Both coaches are of the low voltage pattern. When first introduced in 1925, they used a system utilizing the ordinary house supply of electricity for both powering trains and lights. These coaches can be identified by the little insulated blocks with two terminals in the shape of small sockets in which cords linked the two adjacent vehicles.

122. The first type of No. 2 Luggage Van.

123. The No. 2 Cattle Truck of later date.

124. The G.W. Luggage Van with gold letter transfers of the early 1930's.

125. An early Cattle Truck with white letters.

126. Final design of the No. 2 Luggage Van, the post war version, with a lamp iron at each end.

127. Final pre-war design with gold letters and auto-couplings.

128. On the left, an early Trolley Wagon with convenient slotted base for carrying another wagon.

129. Below, the No. 2 Timber Truck with the load of three pieces of wood. There were many miles of timber used in this fashion.

130. Left. A Crane Truck of the early 1930's with shaded letters and hook couplings. The Van would have looked more prototypical if the roof had been fitted with the chimney as with the Brake Van.

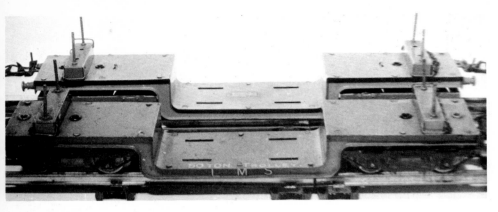

131. *The Trolley Wagons on the left have different couplings: hook type, and automatic furthest from the camera which have the bogie restricting tabs inboard of the pivot.*

132. *Left, another two versions of the same wagon. Intentional or not, the stantions to hold the load are pressed away from the chassis in opposite directions, but are still concave when viewed from the wagon side.*

Shortly after the introduction of the first Pullman Coach came the bogie goods stock. Quickly four vehicles were available and were shorter in length than the passenger stock and were mounted on 2 four-wheeled bogie trucks. A Box Van with double doors opening in the centre of each side was called the No. 2 Luggage Van and it said so on the side. (*Plate 122*). There was a close relative in the No. 2 Cattle Track. A Breakdown Van and Crane and a Trolley Wagon made up the quartet. The Trolley Wagon was slightly longer on account of the depressed centre section, which had four slots in the base. The purpose of these slots caused a considerable amount of speculation as to their use. *Plate 128* may help to solve that problem. The No. 2 Timber Wagon and the No. 2 Lumber Wagon followed and were the same length as the Trolley Wagon. By a year or so later both had "younger brothers" in the four wheeled range. Three slats of timber or five poles were provided as a load for these respective wagons. *Plate 132* shows a common error found on the Timber Wagon. These six wagons were the mainstay of the bogie goods stock for many years, changing colour from time to time. At one period the Lumber Wagon was painted in a colour that was anything but railwaylike, being bright yellow with light green bogie and bolsters. Later, in the years just before the War the six were joined by a No. 2 High Capacity Wagon, three versions were available at 4/- each. A red livery for the L.N.E.R. carried Bricks from Fletton. The G.W. and the L.M.S. carried Loco Coal. Appropriate loads could be bought for these wagons, 6d. for the Loco Coal which was black dyed cork, or for 10d. a box of 100 red bricks as a load for the

L.N.E.R. The Southern Railway drew a blank with the High Capacity Wagon, this may have been due once more to the War halting production. Of the stocks of parts used up after the War those for the High Capacity Wagon are thought to have been used for the L.M.S. version. The Luggage Van returned in a brown livery with small white letters for L.M.S., S.R. or L.N.E.R. Only a minor detail distinguished them from the pre-war vans, and that was the inclusion of a lamp iron in the centre of the end panels. The Well or Trolley Wagon was produced for a short while, until the parts "cold stored" were used up. Before leaving the eight-wheeled goods stock mention should be made that the Trolley Wagon was also available with two cable drums at 4/6d., which was 6d. more than the empty version.

All the bogie vehicles were designed to be used on the 2ft. radius curved track, this caption accompanied any advertisement for bogie stock, which was a little disheartening for the lad with everything except 2ft. curves. Later versions which were fitted with automatic couplings had a slightly modified bogie to carry the controlling wire to keep the couplings in line with the centre of the curved track. A small tongue protruding through an arc in the body prevented the bogie from swivelling too far and causing damage to the bogie or coupling.

All of the many hundred parts used in the making of the Hornby trains were designed, made and assembled by a work force of over 1000 persons. They made their way by foot, bicycle or tram to be at Binns Road by 7.30 a.m. for those whose work was in the factory, or 9 a.m.

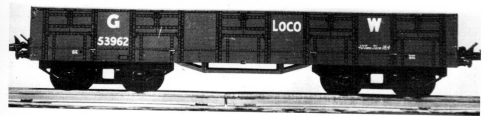

133. The final design of bogie Goods Vehicles. The G.W. and L.M.S. were lithographed in grey. Both carried coal, bought as an extra.

133a. The close-up picture on the right shows the makers transfer used during the 1930's. On life size versions this would have been the makers own metal works plate.

134. The L.N.E.R. version was printed in brick red; a load of bricks being available at extra cost. The Wagon on the left has been fitted with a new set of spoked wheels; the originals having deteriorated as many did of those made in the late 1930's due to impurities in the alloy used.

for those whose tasks fell into the category of "White Collar Workers". Mr. Frank Hornby usually arrived at ten, having been driven to the factory in his Rolls Royce motor car.

One particular morning he arrived as usual and went up to his office. There was as usual waiting on his desk those items which required his attention, the latest "figures" for his perusal, and his personal mail. His attention was drawn from his desk, perhaps he was thinking about his favourite sister, Martha, whose farm he visited the day before. If she knew he was coming she would prepare a particular delicacy of his, Buttermilk with knobs of butter, of which he had been known to drink a quart at a sitting. Whatever the cause of his contemplation, he sent one of the girl messengers to ask his nephew Willie to "Step up and see me". So Bill set off to see what was required of him, and upon entering the great man's office inquired of his Uncle's need of him. "Sit down, Willie" replied Uncle Frank, "How long does it take you to get here by nine in the morning?" "About an hour and a half, Uncle", for the young man came into Liverpool from an address on the Wirral Peninsular, via Rock Ferry and the Mersey Underground Railway to Exchange Station, where he then rode the tram out to the Old Swan area. Uncle Frank sat and listened as the journey was explained and then he said quite casually, "Well take your time and get here by nine thirty". Oh dear, there could be trouble around the offices when this news was spread by the gossips. However there was quiet and every one seemed to accept outwardly that if Mr. Hornby said so then everything was in order. This perquisite was however soon to be replaced with

another generous gesture by Uncle Frank. For there was in certain quarters no such placid acceptance to his bending the rules for one of his relatives. Voices of disapproval could be heard in executive places. Confronted with this disconcertment, and being a dogged man determined that he would have his way in any matter, he did concede that for the sake of harmony on the office floor that nine in the morning was nine and not nine thirty, but at the point of telling Bill that he would have to get in on time in future Frank said that he would pay for a Taxi to be at the Exchange Station every morning to bring Willie and his other two nephews, the fourth seat being occupied by a clerk who had been in Hornby's employ since the James Street days. This Taxi was hired for the trip in the morning and returning at the end of the days work.

This arrangement was to run for many years summer and winter, when the mode of travel was especially welcome. No more was there a need to queue in the rain for the tram that never seemed to come when most needed. Following Mr. Hornby's death the Company Secretary took it upon himself to cancel the order for the Taxi, for it was the Company that had been paying the account, and not as the recipients had thought, their Uncle. The thought of leaving the factory as previously, on foot, amid the bicycles and the masses making for the trams was too much for the quartet on top of their sudden bereavement. They had a hasty conference, decided upon a course of action and making a telephone call rehired the Taxi, paying the fare themselves which amounted to about 10/- each per week, and was worth every penny of it.

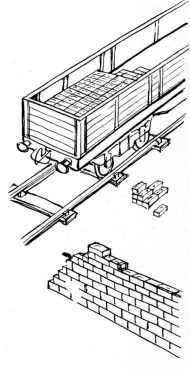

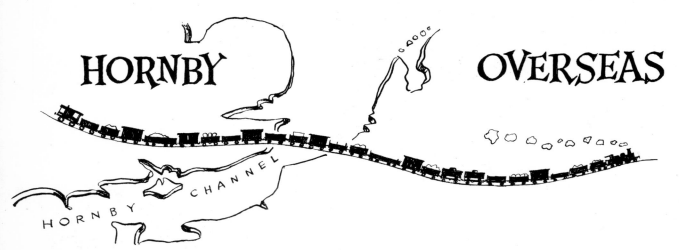

HORNBY OVERSEAS

To appreciate the position of Hornby Trains overseas, consideration to how the market was derived should be given. Meccano created the market and as appreciation of the educational merit of the toy subsequently increased so the factory was finding difficulty in keeping abreast of the demand. Orders which came not only from the British Empire where emissaries of trade had expounded the virtues of the new kind of toy to those exiled from their native homeland, but from parts of the world which were not part of King Edward's or King George's Dominions overseas; countries where English was hardly spoken. To help overcome this linguistic problem Hornby had by 1912 the instruction manuals printed in French, Spanish, Chinese and Russian. There were supply problems and Hornby proposed that in 1913 he would open branches to his business in France, Germany and in the United States of America, a country where a few years earlier Hornby had fought a law suit to protect his invention.

The American Branch was known as "Meccano Inc." with a Registered Office in the Masonic Hall, with other premises at 71 West 23rd Street, also at 46 West 24th Street in New York. The Factory was accommodated in a two story building containing an area of 35,000 sq.ft. situated at 1004, Elizabeth Avenue, Elizabeth, New Jersey. The Company worked against much opposition as national tendencies favoured the American toy makers. Firstly Meccano was made and distributed as the sole product, but in later years Hornby introduced the Trains and a modest Locomotive made suitable for the 10 cent stores. There was also some Rolling Stock, similar to the "American" pattern of stock made at Liverpool. It was distinguished from the British version by the decal HORNBY LINES as opposed to the more familiar HORNBY SERIES. By 1931 business in the U.S.A. had caused Frank Hornby to cross the Atlantic a total of 60 times, many being in connection with the Patents Infringement case. After Hornby's death the American factory continued to make and distribute the Hornby products, but the event of the Second World War caused the company to cease production and to put the factory up for sale in 1940.

The Branch to be established in Germany was to be of great importance. For many years the German Toy Industry had made the best toys of a mechanical nature and had enjoyed a liberal market in the British Isles. Now with his Invention protected by Patents Hornby anticipated there would be a welcome market in Germany for the construction toy. He was to be proved correct, and but for that tragic day in August 1914 would have continued to supply young Hans with his toys. The factory of the German Branch was situated in Berlin, the precise location has now faded along with the Kaiser's Reich, but the Registered Office of Meccano Gesellschaft mbH was in Burohaus Borse, Burgstrasse 28 Berlin. In the "Zentrum" district of those former days in the City. The Burgstrasse runs alongside the River Spree, and is in the terms of today's administration in the Berlin-Mitte district. In 1916 the Company had a registered Director in a Mr. J. P. Porteus and although it is thought that Frank's younger son Douglas, a fluent German linguist was working in the German Company as the man in charge it is unlikely that he remained in Germany after 1914. Under powers given to themselves the Central State Authorities took over many companies owned by foreign nationals and appointed Managers. In some instances due to a decree issued in 1916 the Central State Authority was empowered to "wind up" any foreign owned business, so hardly had production started when the factory was commandeered and used for the production of munitions for the ensuing years. When hostilities ceased Frank Hornby and his Company Meccano Ltd. were entitled to reclaim their former property, now classified as War Reparations. Hornby felt he could not trade with the former enemy and sold the factory complete with any of the original machine tools, stock, and materials that the munition workers had left behind, to Gebruder Märklin. The Brothers Märklin used the tools to make their own construction system under their own name, but which in effect was the same as the contemporary Meccano. In later years when feelings over the war had mellowed a little an Agency was established in Munich with Douglas taking charge once more.

Paris was the site chosen for the Mecca of Hornby in France. It was intended to supply all the needs of the French Market and those of the French Colonies. The factory was situated at 78—80 Rue Rebeval, Bobigny (Seine) with an office at 5, Rue Ambroise Thomas, Paris. Firstly only Meccano was made but in the early 1920's the factory was tooled up for the production of trains. Hornby sent his elder son, Roland, to be Manager-in-Charge for a while, "As it would be an advantage to have a member of the Family there to look after things, and any way it would help him with his French", which he spoke fluently. The Factory continued to support the good name of Meccano on the Continent giving Pierre the guarantee he needed to buy the Trains Hornby when they were first put on sale in the Paris shops. The Trains that he was able to buy bearing the label "Fab Par Meccano Paris" were locomotives coaches and wagons that were basically the same as those made in Liverpool, but painted in the liveries of the four great French Railways, NORD; EST; ETAT; and P.L.M. The British boy was familiar with NORD for he had seen it on a limited number of wagons made in Liverpool, but the remainder were new to him. Hopper, Side and Rotary Wagons, the Fibre Wagons with P.L.M. on the side. The private owners wagon "FYFFES" was there just the same, but the British Biscuit Wagons were replaced with "HUNTLEY & PALMERS", which was not available here. A "UNION" Refrigerator Van and two types of Petrol/Oil Tankers were also new to the English boy. The standard No. 2 Goods Wagons were made in the liveries of the four French main lines and some were supplied with the Brakeman's Hut seen on the British version of the NORD wagon, officially referred to as a Guerite. The Paris factory survived the two wars and was only closed in recent years.

The market which Meccano established in the British Empire and in Countries outside were eager to accept the Hornby Trains and to meet these orders the standard liveried trains of the day were exported. This may have warmed the heart of the exiled Derby man to see a Midland Train Set 3000 miles from home,

135. The first of three models from the French factory. On the left is the Travelling Post Office, although the prototype had eight wheels. A British version would have been welcome.

136. The Double Wine Wagon on the right is from the post war production line.

137. Finally, the Golden Arrow Coach which has the same structure as the No. 2 Special Pullman, but with the cant rail title of the 'Blue Coaches'.

but it did little for the New Zealander who was now inquiring into the possibility of buying his locomotive with N.Z.R. emblazoned on the tender. Eager to satisfy his new customers Hornby had the initials of local companies transferred and placed on the locomotives which were painted in the standard colours of the British main lines. There was in addition the opportunity for the overseas customer to order many of the standard range of locomotives in a black livery. Agencies were established in the Dominion Countries of New Zealand, Australia, South Africa, India, and many of the Foreign Kingdoms and Republics. One such Agent, that of Italy, made part of his social season to visit England and to go to the Meccano Factory to meet Frank Hornby. Others less fortunate due mainly to the lengthy sea journey awaited the arrival of the Steamer for their supplies of Meccano, Hornby Train sets, and the Meccano Magazine with editions printed in French and Spanish. These were for the South American market which in 1932 could boast ten Agents in the Territories excluding Argentina, where details of

Dealers and Agents have now merged with the mists of time. Most were centred in the capital city of Buenos Aires City and the Capital Province, but some could be found in the principal towns of 8 of the 23 provinces. Of all of the overseas countries to be supplied with the Trains painted in the local liveries the South American Continent appears to have been most patronised with the Railways of the Argentina Republic being made as early as 1925. Four of the main lines were available using again the British main line colours to represent Argentinian Railways which had at that time majority share-holders in the United Kingdom. The L.M.S. Red was lettered F.C.S. and became a locomotive on the Ferrocarril Sud, while the L.N.E.R. Green and lettered F.C.O. ran on the Ferrocarril Oeste, the West railway. Southern Green livery ran for the F.C.C.A. in the Central Argentine, whilst it is thought that the British G.W. locomotives were lettered F.C.B.A.P. for the Buenos Aires to Pacific Railway, although there is little evidence today for only a small batch of F.C.B.A.P. rolling stock appears to have been made.

138. No. 2 Special Tank
Locomotive in the South
American livery of
F.C.S.

139. Left we see one of the
early export wagons on
type 1 chassis with hook
couplings and F.C.B.A.P.
initials, rare in 1924.

140. On the right, the No. 1
Luggage Van with white
letters mounted on
type 3 chassis.

141. An early open wagon on
type 2 chassis. Another
well-used vehicle judging
by the lack of paint
remaining after 40 years!

142. The wagon 'B' in the
colours of the
FerroCarril Sud.

143. The photograph on the
left was taken in Buenos
Aires, but since then the
wagon has returned to
this country and is now
in the Author's
collection.

144. With just a change of initials another model was created, and another boy's wishes satisfied.

145.

Both types of Brake Van, on the left and below, were used for the same railway company.

146.

147. The Crane Truck on the left has the early silver wheels, but has lost the hook and cord over the years.

148. Featured on the right is the No. 1 Cattle Truck also from the period of the hook couplings. It has the type 3 chassis with small gold letters.

149. The No. 2 Special Tender, shown here divorced from the Locomotive leaving the reader the task of fitting the correct engine.

150. The No. 1 Luggage Van of the F.C.C.A. helps illustrate the extent of the demands of the South American market.

151. The Cement Wagon was an early type in the Hornby Series.

152. The L.N.E.R. type Brake Van in service in South America.

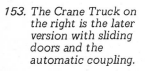

153. The Crane Truck on the right is the later version with sliding doors and the automatic coupling.

153a. F.C.O. No. 2 Luggage Van version for the French Lines had the brakeman's hut on some of the No. 2 Goods Wagons.

154. The brown livery of the Riviera 'Blue' Locomotive is seen here with an E.S.R. Tender; the serial number however, is the same.

LOCOMOTIVES

Hornby stressed to all concerned that a high standard of workmanship was to be put into the construction of the clockwork motor, designed for the new product, the Hornby Train. The factory had some experience of clockwork mechanisms, but as this was to be a new venture extra care was to be exercised to insure that the engines ran well. Little could Hornby have thought that as a result of all that care there would be locomotives running 50 years after their manufacture.

It was fitting that a company which marketed a construction toy would apply the same principle to the new toy, and therefore locomotives and wagons could at first be taken to pieces. Spare parts were available to replace any which may have been damaged by rough usage. The first locomotives were small four wheeled types with four wheeled tenders, mostly painted black but red and blue could be seen on slightly later versions. The enormous success of the new Train Sets soon gave Hornby the enthusiasm to set about introducing another, larger engine. This engine was fitted with a more powerful mechanism. The length was increased to enable a four wheeled bogie to be fitted under the smoke box, and a six wheeled tender was more in proportion than the older four wheeled version. Known as the No. 2 Locomotive, it was available in black presumably to represent the L.N.W.R., in red for the Midland Railway, in green for the Great Northern Railway, and in blue for the Caledonian Railway. The remaining Railway Company of the first five, the London, Brighton and South Coast Railway, does not appear to have had a livery "allocated", but as the initial letters were not noticable on the locomotives collectors may have chosen colours to suit their favourite line.

Moving on a few years, locomotives were now available in the colours of the newly formed L.M.S. and L.N.E.R. companies, and later in the liveries of the G.W. and Southern Railways. Also introduced was a Tank Engine version of the No. 2 Locomotive with the rather unusual wheel arrangement of 4-4-4. This robust and likeable engine had the same clockwork mechanism as the tender version.

The next major development in the Locomotive Section was the introduction of electricity as the prime mover. Hornby's products were designed to meet the requirements of a "Good Clientele", the customer whose house was now being wired for electric light in the mid 1920's. For this customer Hornby made a locomotive to be driven by electricity. It had been generally accepted that in this small gauge (O) the best medium for their propulsion was clockwork, although there were some steam driven locomotives made by other manufacturers. Hornby had not thought there was a need to change this general arrangement, until now. Electricity was to be the power, therefore why not have an Electric Locomotive? A revelation indeed. But where was there a prototype locomotive that did not look like a railway carriage or did not come from a foreign country? The large BO-BO locomotive of the London Metropolitan Railway was the answer.

As accurate as possible was the word sent down, and as accurate as possible was the design. The fact that the locomotive had only four wheels was hidden by the valance sheets below the running plate which were embossed with the bogie design of the prototype. The electric motor was made to work in

"Series" with a rheostat and a 60 watt electric light bulb all being connected to the 230 Volts house supply. The system worked well and has been used on numerous occasions where all the components are in fixed positions, however when the locomotive became derailed or was removed from the track the power and return rails became charged to the same voltage as the supply and could be very dangerous if touched by hand. It was perfectly safe if the supply was switched off before re-railing the locomotive, but the risk, thought Hornby, was too great and so the locomotive was redesigned to work off the much lower power of 4 volts.

The High or House Voltage locomotive, the new coaches and the electric track were all ready for the Christmas season of 1925, and cost £5/10/-, which must have been considered by many as expensive, but then it was a new toy and the latest from HORNBY! Later, for those who wanted the latest but whose home was not electrically lit there was a clockwork version of the electric outline locomotive using the mechanism designed for the No. 2 Locomotive. The later low voltage locomotive had the advantage of being able to work satisfactorily from a 4 volt Accumulator should "Mains" not be available..

155. This small locomotive was a non-reversing type, and was available in red or green; costing 3/9d.

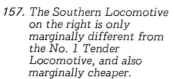

156. The No. 1 Tender Locomotive (minus Tender here) is in the L.M.S. livery and still has the flat bulb head lamp.

157. The Southern Locomotive on the right is only marginally different from the No. 1 Tender Locomotive, and also marginally cheaper.

158. Some of the details of the Hornby Electric Motor can be seen here. At the top left is the hand reversing lever. The cage in the centre has the armature bearing, and on 20-volt auto reversing motors hold part of the reversing lever. Note the thickness of the running wheel bearings.

159. Not all Hornby Trains were in the hands of the boys. The photo on the right shows a post-war M.1 Engine in red livery which after many years' service on a girl's model railway was just as good as when new.

160. The locomotive No.50153 on the left is also a post-war engine in the 501 Series and very similar to the pre-war No. 1 Locomotives. There was a green (passenger) and a black (goods) version of what must be the last of a very long line of Hornby Locomotives.

161. In the terms of the motor car salesman, the above is a 'one-owner' model. This M.3 Tank Engine was purchased in 1935.

162. Above is an early Southern No. 1 Tank Engine rescued from the knackers yard still carrying a pretentious head code.

163. On the left is a type 101 of early post-war days and looks very similar to the pre-war No. 1 Tank Engines of which *plate 164* is a well-used Southern Locomotive version.

164. Despite the winder spigot being off centre No. E 126 still runs well.

165. Another early No. 1 Tank Locomotive, on the left, still proudly carrying the express head code. One of the features of this model was the dome in polished metal instead of being painted.

166. No. 2 Locomotive in black livery and numbered 2711. Other liveries were red, green and blue.

167. This locomotive should be in the "Hornby Overseas" section as the Engine was made in the Paris factory. It carries the initials of the Paris, Lyon & Marseille Railway. The livery whether correct or not is maroon, similar to the L.M.S. colour.

168. The above insert photograph shows the Makers transfer used on the products of the Paris factory.

169. Left, a clockwork G.W.R. version of the No. 2 Special Tank Locomotive, clearly showing the track control levers adjacent to the driving wheels.

170. Right, the L.N.E.R. model in black livery was the 'Goods' loco; the green version being for 'Passenger' services.

171. A later version of the No. 2 Locomotive having the L.M.S. red livery.

172. This No. 1 Tank Locomotive was a fine engine with a long run per winding. Only first available in L.M.S. or L.N.E.R. styling later models appeared in G.W.R. and S.R. liveries. They were very similar to an earlier Hornby unit called a Zulu Tank Engine. There was also a Zulu Tender Locomotive and the apparent difference was that the Zulu Trains were slightly cheaper. However, by about 1925 they were replaced by the No. 0 range of locomotives.

173. On the right is the L. & N.E.R. version of the No. 2 Tank Locomotive, which is a little earlier than the L.N.E.R. model. Note that the running number is identical with the wheel arrangement.

174. Left, another No. 2 Tank Engine in the dark green of the Great Western Railway; the length being 11½in. and costing 32/6d in 1925. The lettering appears somewhat large.

175. By the time the Southern version, right, was introduced, the Design Department had given running numbers which did not coincide with the wheel arrangement.

176. No excuse is offered for yet another No. 2 model, as these splendid engines emphasise the care that Hornby put into the manufacture of their products. These models were photographed after 45 years of service.

178. Underside of the Metropolitan Electric Locomotive, showing the four driving wheels and current collecting shoes.

177. A close-up of the popular Metropolitan Electric Locomotive. The lever at the right of the cab door controls the power to the large flat headlight bulb. A similar arrangement existed at the other end. The reversing lever can be seen below the lamp, minus the milled brass knob originally supplied.

179. A three quarter view of the Locomotive.

179a. Left, insert photo of the 'MET' Coat of Arms, much enlarged.

180. General view of the Metropolitan Locomotive showing the excellent detail. The deep skirting at each side cleverly disguised the large wheels.

Success was to follow with more loco-motives, this time to suit the new French train being introduced — The RIVIERA BLUE — as it was called unofficially. The locomotive had an Atlantic wheel arrangement and the bodywork resembled a locomotive of the French NORD Railway. It was completed with an 8 wheeled tender. This locomotive was available with the clockwork mechanism or the 4 volt electric motor. The basic parts produced for the NORD locomotive were used the following year to make another locomotive, this time of British outline and still in the 4-4-2 wheel category, and given the colours of the four main lines. Each carried the name of one of the well-known engines of those lines. The disappointing aspect of these names was that the prototype locomotives all had different wheel notation from that used by Hornby. The four engines were named "Flying Scotsman"; "Royal Scot"; "Caerphilly Castle" and "Lord Nelson".

Complaints which came to the notice of the Hornby Company were always noted and when the opportunity arose to make another model any improvements which could be made without incurring too much additional expense were always considered. There had been many requests for more realistic locomotives, as the Metropolitan was, but in steam outline. The chance to make a more realistic locomotive came when Hornby introduced plans for a 4-4-0 locomotive and tender. The L.N.E.R. had just built the first of the "Yorkshire" class engines, naming the first No. 234, "Yorkshire". Topical as always, Hornby's L.N.E.R. 4-4-0 was aptly named "Yorkshire". Later when the L.N.E.R. built a similar class of "Hunt" locomotives, Hornby changed the name of their locomotive to No. 201 "Bramham Moor" the first locomotive of the proto-type class. The L.M.S. and the Southern Railway versions were models of unnamed prototypes, the Great Western one was of the "County" class and was named "County of Bedford". All were "true-to-type" and had tenders to suit and whilst it was the intention that these engines and tenders were to be used as one unit it was always possible to purchase them as separate items, the locomotive was £1/2/6d. and the tender 5/6d. At first these true to types were only made with the new No. 2 Special Clockwork mechanism but later versions were fitted with the 20 volt electric motor.

As a contemporary to the No. 2 Special tender locomotive Hornby produced the No. 2 Special Tank engine. This was not so prototypical but nevertheless was a powerful engine of the 4-4-2 wheel arrange-ment. This came at the same price as the tender version, less of course, the price of the tender. This again was at first only available in clockwork. The new, more

powerful, locomotive spelt the end of the demand for the old 4-4-4 No. 2 Tank engine, and with the plant at Binns Road tooled up for a continuous run on the parts for the older tank engine, it was duly redesigned. By using the clockwork mechanism made for the 4-4-4 and a newly designed body, Hornby introduced a No. 1 Special Tank engine, costing 16/6d. it was an 0-4-0 and slightly larger than the existing 0-4-0 locomotives.

The younger users of model railways were not forgotten by Hornby and for these children small four wheeled loco-motives in bright red or green were made and classed as M1., they were powered by clockwork and were non-reversing. For very young brothers or sisters there was by 1932 the M.O. engine, mounted on four wheels and with the key permanently attached. This too was available in red or green and carried the running numbers of two of the most famous steam engines, numbers 4472 and 6100.

The electric motors were wound to work as has been observed on 4 volts. Later as the popularity of electricity spread 6 volt and 20 volt motors were made. Whilst these motors were intended to use Alternating Current from the mains supply via a transformer, they would if required work from an accumulator. An automatic reversing device had been invented for use with the 20 volt motor, which operated when the supply was switched on and caused the engine to move in one direction, the supply then switched off and on again caused the engine to move in the opposite direction. This gave a considerable increase in the realistic operation of the locomotive. However, should the collecting shoe lose contact with the power rail, as could happen at a point or damaged section of track, the automatic switch would operate and reverse the direction of the locomotive. Hornby appreciated that this switch could sometimes be a little more automatic than was really desired and provided a locking lever which enabled the user to choose when automatic reversing was required. Another feature of the electric powered engines was that many were fitted with a headlight, placed, as can be seen in the photographs, in the centre of the smoke box door, and looking very much out of place. When the No. 2 Special Tender Locomotive became well established thoughts were turned to producing another true to type locomotive range.

It was a formidable task to keep abreast of the innovations of the Main Railway Companies, but one man was able to do this, for he held the position of Advertising Manager and that of Editor of the Meccano Magazine. In this position he was on very good terms with the Press Relations Officers on the Main Railway Companies. These P.R.O.'s kept him

informed on any new developments and with a staff of loyal subordinates he had been able to produce many of the ideas which subsequently became models in the Hornby Series. Mr. McCormick, the "Ideas Man", on one particular morning was full of enthusiasm. Instructing one of his assistants to get a draughtsman and the Company Photographer, the four men left the factory by car for the railway sidings at Edge Hill, only one knowing the purpose of their mission. Upon arrival the purpose was revealed, for standing there was the new L.M.S. Express engine No. 6201, "Princess Elizabeth". Now here was a find for any loco-spotter. Officially it was just resting between duties and the footplate crew were by now accustomed to being inundated by small (and not so small) boys every time their fine engine came to rest. So the sight of four more "boys" descending upon them did not cause them to seek sanctuary behind the DO NOT TRESPASS ON THE RAILWAY notice, even if they were carrying a camera, a roll of drawings, tape measure and similar apparel. Could it have been that the crew had been advised that they might be invaded by some Liverpudlians? The team measured this and photographed that, and made quick sketches of certain parts to which Mr. McCormick directed their attention. When the team departed from the sidings that day they had sufficient information to enable the Company to set up plant to construct a model of the crack express engine of the L.M.S. There were some new features for Hornby to consider, until now all the mechanisms had been of four driving wheels, now one with six was required. Most of the other locomotives in Hornby's range used some common parts, even the true to type series had many parts of common use, but here was an entirely new engine. The finished locomotive was supplied complete with tender in a presentation box at £5/5/-. When the driver of the real "Princess Elizabeth" was asked what he thought of the Hornby model, Mr. Clarke is quoted as saying, "It's fine". The more realistic locomotive story does not quite end there, for returning to the 4-4-0 wheeled engines Hornby decided to produce a model of the Southern Railways "Schools" class. It is doubtful if the same technique for obtaining the details was used as with the "Princess Elizabeth", but a fine detailed locomotive was made and offered to the public for 50/- electric or 43/- clockwork. Named ETON the engine was painted in the correct colours and carried No. 900 on the tender. Had the war of 1939 not caused production to cease there could have been plans for a scale model of the L.N.E.R. 4472 "Flying Scotsman" and who knows maybe one of the Great Western "Kings".

181. This 3.E Locomotive named "LORD NELSON" has the early tender as used on the No. 2 Tender Locomotives.

182. A closer view of the same locomotive. Rather grotesque and non-railway like, in reality "LORD NELSON" had a 4-6-0 type wheel arrangement and not a 4-4-2 'Atlantic' type wheel base.

183. The picture on the right shows the improvements made by the smoke deflectors and re-styled tender.

184. Left shows, in close-up, the valve gear and name on the leading splasher. Other names used in the Loco No. 3 range were "ROYAL SCOT" of the L.M.S.; "FLYING SCOTSMAN" for the L.N.E.R., and "CAERPHILLY CASTLE" representing the G.W.R.

185. There was a considerable improvement in realism with the 'true to type' Hornby models. On the right we see No. 234 "YORKSHIRE" of the L.N.E.R.

186. Left, shows the Great Western model of No. 3821 "COUNTY OF BEDFORD". There was a true likeness with tapered boiler and small cab as seen on G.W.R. locos.

187. On the right is yet another clockwork powered 'true to type' model this time in L.M.S. colours and general outline of a Compound Locomotive.

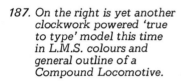

188. Left we see a three quarter view of the Southern Railway version, which included accurate tender details for each type of model.

189. When the L.N.E.R. introduced the 'Hunt' class, Hornby had the "YORKSHIRE" model re-styled to become No. 201 "THE BRAMHAM MOOR".

190. *Enter the Streamliners! On the left, the "SILVER JUBILEE" train. It was only available with a clockwork motor.*

190a. *On the right, is a later maroon and cream train, and there was also a two-tone green version. These were introduced to help use the parts fashioned for a long run of the "SILVER JUBILEE" which did not materialise.*

Whilst in the Locomotive Department, an idea to help sell the latest engines was devised and called the Exchange System. This scheme was for the owners of older locomotives to return their engine to the Company to be given an allowance against the purchase price of a new engine. An example was that 11/3d. was allowed as the trade-in price on the old No. 2 Tank engine, the only condition being that the new locomotive must cost at least double the allowance. Most of the changes and news of new or improved models were made in the Meccano Magazine which had grown from a simple sheet introduced in 1916 to a complete Boys Magazine with features on many non-railway and non-Meccano activities such as stamp collecting; books to read; photography, and many similar hobbies. All the Meccano products were advertised and other manufacturers goods were also advertised provided they were not likely to hinder sales of the Meccano products. One such advertiser had the locomotive depicted on page 57 as the "Challenger" displayed at a price that made the German locomotive very competitive. Even the Readers Column of Advertisements was subject to scrutiny and only advertisements without the word HORNBY were usually accepted. The Exchange Scheme was discontinued at the outbreak of war and not re-introduced afterwards as there were few new engines.

Of the locomotives that were made after the war only the small four wheeled variety were produced in any quantities as the shortages of materials was acute and again the popular demand for the smaller "OO" gauge trains took precedence. One other noticeable change was the replacement of the pre-war classification by a type number. With all of these changes there was no change in the appeal to children, the Hornby Train was still popular, for now the parents who were the pre-war children remembered how much enjoyment they had from their Hornby Train. The magic was, however, to move into the field of plastics and smaller places to keep trains, and so "OO" took over completely.

191. *The No. 1 Special Tank Engine had a cousin in the No. 1 Special Tender Locomotive. These powerful four-wheeled engines had the same mechanism as the old No. 2 Tanks, suitably modified to fit. The one shown here is clockwork, but there were 20-volt electric versions.*

192. Left is the only example of the No. 4 series made. Possibly the fore-runner of another 'true to type' series, "ETON" was available with a 20-volt electric or clockwork power unit.

193. On the right is an early "NORD". Latter versions had smoke deflectors. This photograph was taken under running conditions at an Annual General Meeting of the Hornby Railway Collectors Association.

194. Referred to in these pages as the Challenger this Marklin 4-4-0 type Locomotive was one of many advertised in the Meccano Magazine by retailers. Costing about 57/6d. this locomotive came equipped with two electrically-lit headlamps.

195. The 'Piece de resistance' of the Hornby range of locomotives, shown here without the tender. Many of the engines of this period had wheels made of alloy containing some impurities. This caused the wheels to deteriorate sooner than some of the older locomotives. This example has been fitted with a new set of wheels.

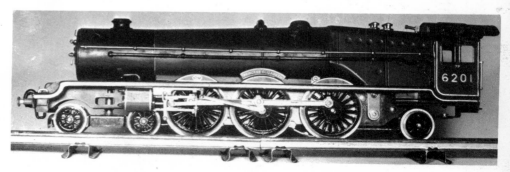

Few model railway manufacturers advertised that their system could be said to be complete. Hornby could, for all the usual paraphernalia of the railway scene could be supplied in miniature, some in reasonable scale, and others in out of gauge proportions. In addition to the range of accessories there was also a range of Complete Model Railways. These consisted of a basic train set with such accessories as a station, tunnel, signal box, trees and two animals. All were housed in a special strong box, and these complete model railways made an excellent Christmas present and a good starting point to the great game of train running.

Perhaps the best place to start a review of the accessories is at the largest of the stations which measured 2'9" in length, constructed in tinplate with the station scene lithographed on the building. The basic scene did not change over the years, but the costumes of the people kept abreast of the fashions, whilst the motor cars in the "through the arch" street scene were often updated. The opening doors to the various "rooms" gave way to the printed form, and the miniature candle holders, a feature of both Hornby and contemporary Continental stations, were omitted. One feature which did not alter was the height of the platform, it stayed at the apparent lower than scale height for the British level of 4'1". To lengthen the station or to fabricate more complicated main line termini, extension platforms and island platforms were also available. For more modest layouts, and supplied in the Complete Model Railways, were smaller wayside stations, a "Town Station" and a country halt very similar to Ulting Halt on the Maldon branch in Essex, past which the writer travelled on many occasions each of which saw no train standing at the platform. Most of the accessories had indentifying numbers, the No. 1 being considered as standard and No. 2 the more superior. Stations, however, rose to 4 with those of latter date being fitted with electric light which were identified by adding an "E" after the number. An "E" before a title indicated the item was designed for use on electric track. The tinplate Goods Depot was available in two sizes after the original goods depot was made by adapting the early island platform. Signal boxes came in two types plus the "E" version. Signals were in several patterns, a splendid array of colours and lattice posts surmounted with Home and/or Distance pattern arms. Until quite late in the series the distant arms were red changing only when some of the main line companies introduced yellow painted distant arms. The more superior No. 2 signals were complete with ladders and with ball and spike finials on the earliest types, the later versions having a flat cap type. An exception was the No. 2 Gantry Signal which from its introduction around 1928 was a slow goer, due possibly to the price of 10/-, later 11/6d. which made the first batch of possibly 50,000 last for the duration of the series. By comparison the No. 1 Signal Gantry was a very austere unit.

Telegraph poles; loading gauges; water towers; footbridges; goods yard cranes on plinths; lamp standards carrying one or two lamps, either dummy or electrically lit; tunnels; plate layers huts; fences with or without trees; cuttings; gradient posts; etc., all went to produce the overall picture. There were Engine Sheds to take two small engines or massive tin structures capable of housing two locomotives providing they did not exceed 17½" each in length, and for an extra 2/- at 24/- the engine shed could have an electric light fitted. With all of these accessories the most complete of model railways could be perfected.

The tinplate rails made for the first Hornby Trains bore a resemblance to a Continental pattern, this was useful as there were no patents relating to the track and Hornby's track was able to be used in conjunction with the contemporary rails. However, with the introduction of the electric train Hornby had to redesign his track to include the third rail. The result was a strong but simple design for both electric and clockwork driven trains. Made in tinplate the rail was rolled to the Vignoles section and secured to three sleepers per section. The straight sections were 10¼" long and there were curved sections in 1ft. and 2ft. radii. The two rail track designed for use with clockwork trains had, due to the ingenuity of Hornby, the sleeper sections pierced to allow the inclusion of the centre third rail should the owner wish to convert the track for electric traction at a later date. Double track sections in both straight and 2ft. radius curved pieces and a wide range of points were soon available and once established changed very little. Many pamphlets were provided giving ingenious track layouts using all the pieces available. With the introduction of the M.O. range a new lighter section track was made especially for the range having 9" radius curves and a point of similar radius. As there were no electric M.O. locomotives this track was only made with two rails for clockwork operation. Where points were required with the operating lever placed on the curved side to enable the placing of turnouts in double track sections, these could be obtained by special order. Points suitable for use with the Hornby Control System were also available to order, and as adaptable as always, for those owners who wished to convert existing lever operated points to those of the control system there was the necessary kit of parts.

The new "Princess Elizabeth" locomotive posed a little problem to the staff at Binns Road, for whilst the great engine with the longer than standard wheelbase would negotiate the 2ft. radius curves a curve of larger radii would be more desirable. The design team were not long in producing the answer. A new track of solid steel rail drawn in bullhead section and made in straight sections of 23", with 12 sleepers per section making for a more realistic looking track. The curved sections had a radius of 3ft. and needed ten pieces to form a circle. The only point available was an ordinary turnout made to the length of a half straight with a half curved on the branch. Was a convenient coincidence that two points curve to curve made a crossover at double track spacing? Had it not been for the war other pointwork may have been introduced, but once again the existing layout owner was not forgotten as special adapter pieces at 1/- per box of six were available to make a connection to the tinplate system. Another Track Accessory for the solid steel track was the No.3A Buffer Stop, similar to the No.2A but with solid steel track.

196. Hornby No. 2 Station with opening doors to many rooms. The scene was up-dated from time to time but remained basically the same.

197. The Hornby Station on the right is the No. 4 type with 'walk through arch'. The No. 2 and No. 3 models were similar, but with a printed arch. The 'E' version had two lamp brackets on the corners of the building. The Keyways seen on the platform wall enable the platform extension pieces to be locked together making a one-piece platform of several pieces.

198. For comparison is this German-made Station produced by Bing for the British market. The platform height is similar to the Hornby Stations.

199. Back to the Hornby Series with their Wayside Halt; costing 8d. if purchased separately! It is 9½in. long. There is also a similar station made in France with S.N.C.F. advertisement.

200. This Island Platform is the pre-war version; having lost its WEMBLEY, WINDSOR or BRISTOL sign over the years.

203. The two Painters above, could be seen from many a train window in the years between the wars, and an up-to-date Frank Hornby introduced them into the Dinky Toys range.

TRENT

201. The above post-war Island Platform is shorter in height and has solid pillars.

204. Above we have Porters carrying F.H.'s luggage. Whether the initials were placed there as a result of an instruction or that of an aspiring hand-finisher is not known.

205. Train & Hotel Porters. A set of five cost 1/3d. and came in a box.

202. This No. 2E Goods Depot has sliding doors and the crane slewed 360 degrees. Some of the Hornby Platform Luggage can be seen. The wagon is the 'Serif' version of the Wagon 'B'.

206. Some of the Engineering Staff. The one second from the right has a resemblance to the Station Master of another set, this time wearing a different coat!

207. Above, some of the Station Furniture found on any Hornby Station. Little was left to the imagination.

208. Three views of the Locomotive Lamp, usually supplied with a new Locomotive, but costing 1d. each separately. A similar one was painted red.

209. The Lady Hiker appears to have out-walked her companion from the Complete Model Railway

210. Above, the Station Hoarding Board in post-war buff finish.

210a. Here is the pre-war version which was painted blue.

211. Above we see two No. 2 Engine Sheds supplied with either electric or clockwork track. They each house two No. 3 type Locomotives or four smaller Tank Engines.
Note that the No. E2E Shed on the left is of later manufacture. Gone is the pattern on the inside of the door as with the clockwork track version on the right.

212. Some of the 'M' Station Set which contained two M Signals, two M telegraph poles, one Half-relief Signal Box, Wayside Station and the Town Station. Cost of the set: 2/9d.

Note: The No. 1 Box, of similar dimensions, only had the staircase printed on the side, and the roof did not open.

213. Left, the No. 2 Signal Cabin fitted over the Control System Frame giving an altogether railway appearance. There was also a No. 2E Signal Cabin fitted for electric lighting.

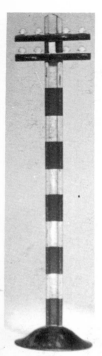
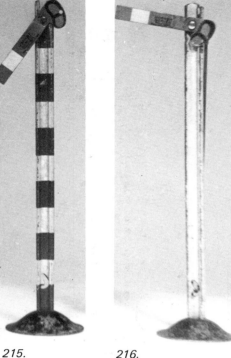

214.   *215.*   *216.*

'M' Telegraph Pole and Signals, rather shorter than the other Hornby Signals the posts were folded into 'Bull-head' rail section as some prototypes. The painting was usually blue and white, but some red and white signal posts have been seen.

217. The No. 2E Double Arm Signal with Electric Lamps. It was also available without the Electric 'E' and the No. 1 versions had no ladder and only a round base.

218. Above, the Junction Signal version with flat-capped finials.

220. Right, a close-up of the Electric Lantern. The lamp top was light tight and gave a realistic light through the coloured spectacle.

221. Below, the complete No. 2E Home Signal. There was also a similar Distant Signal.

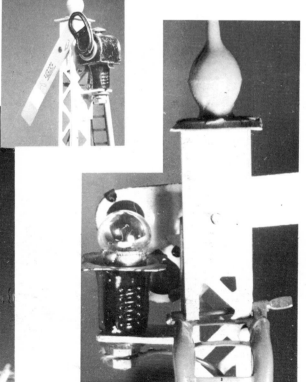

219. The No. 2E Signal Gantry above, had the correct aperture for the rear of the lamp housing, but lacked the moving shade.

222. Left, another close-up of the Electric Lamp, this time with the actual lamp housing removed to show the screw-type bulb.

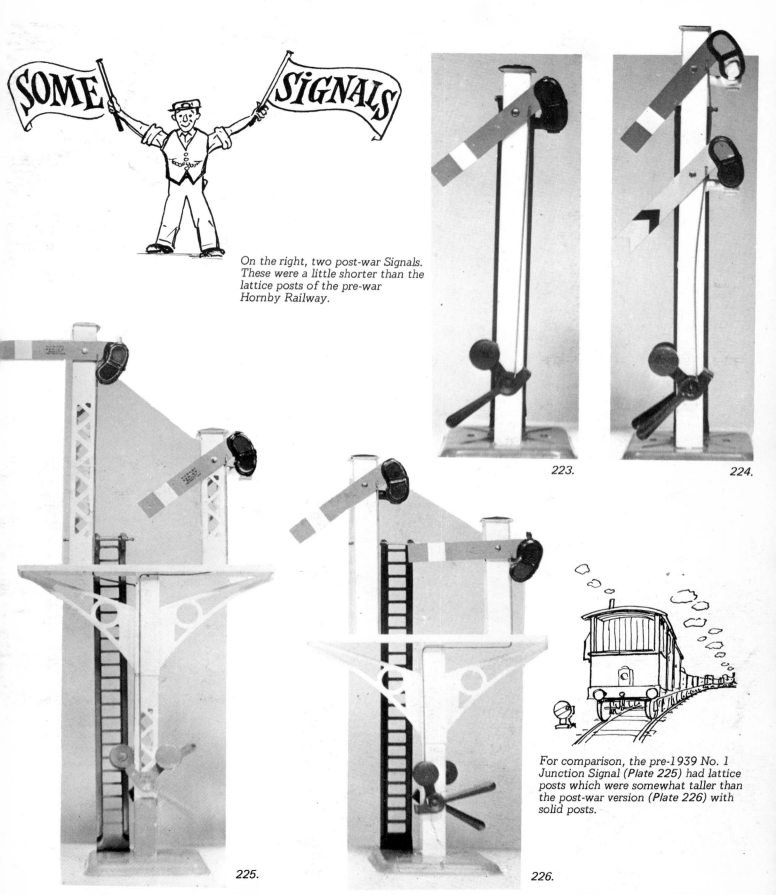

SOME SIGNALS

On the right, two post-war Signals. These were a little shorter than the lattice posts of the pre-war Hornby Railway.

223.

224.

225.

226.

For comparison, the pre-1939 No. 1 Junction Signal (*Plate 225*) had lattice posts which were somewhat taller than the post-war version (*Plate 226*) with solid posts.

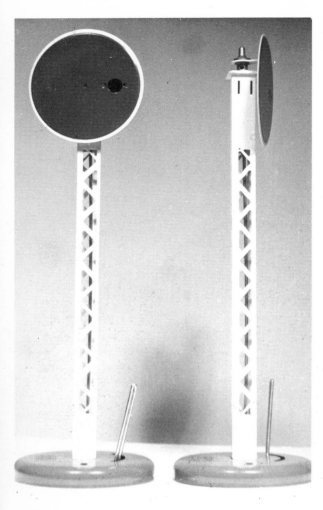

227. Above is a rather nice post-war French Signal, shown at 'danger' and 'off'.

228. Two of the Double Globe Lamp Standards, the left-hand one unlight and now minus one glass globe. The later one on the right is a Electrically-lit pattern.

229. The Water Tower on the far left is a poor example of the pre-war version, minus most of the working parts, which fortunately can be seen on the post-war model standing next to it.

230. Right, is the rather large first type of Water Tower that Hornby made, which has only just survived the ravages of time!

231. The No. 4 Tunnel on the left, designed for 2ft. curved track.

232. Below, is the Metal Tunnel, forerunner of the many wood and cardboard tunnels and cuttings of latter years.

233. Accessories No. 7, complete with outsize shovel and poker. The Shunter's Pole was a separate item at 2d.

234. Below, some of the Track Side Notices. A similar set contained station names, all different

235. The Hornby version of the Lineside Hut. This one has the door printed on the side whereas some others had an opening door. All were far removed from the tarred sleeper-made hovels of the prototypes!

236. The Hornby Viaduct consisted of three track pieces being equal to three straight sections, available with clockwork track or electric.

237. The Centre section could be purchased separately enabling the Viaduct to be extended. Here three such sections are shown together. It is a pity that it was only made for single track.

CROSSINGS

238. The E1 Level Crossing on the left, has a track length equal to half a Straight Rail. Other No. 1 Level Crossings had electric warning lights, one at each gate (designated E1E). A cheaper version was the M0 model; the gates and post being one piece and fitted into holes in the base.

239. The No. 2 Level Crossing on the right, has the length of a full straight and spaced to fit the Double Track sections. There were versions for electric track and also for lights. An older Double Track Level Crossing was for use with Single Track pieces as the spacing was narrower than Double Track Sections.

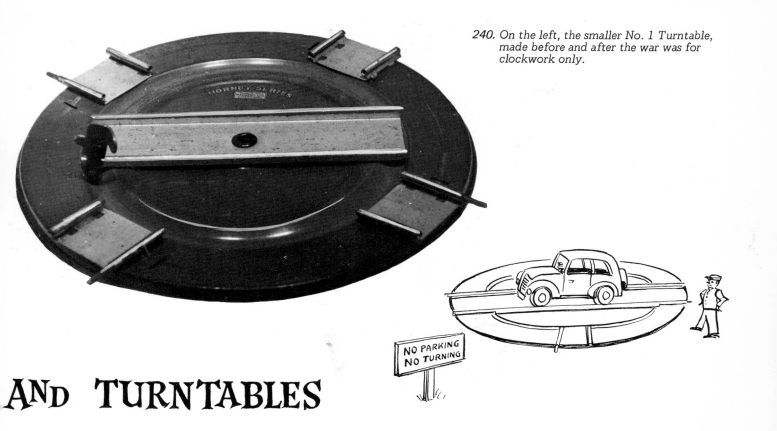

240. On the left, the smaller No. 1 Turntable, made before and after the war was for clockwork only.

AND TURNTABLES

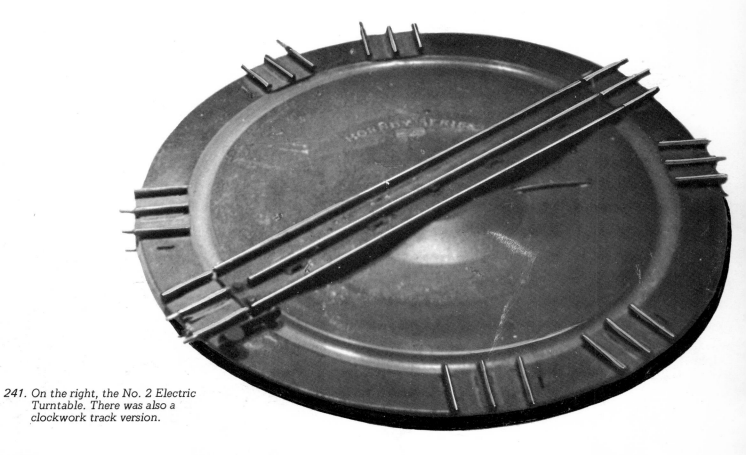

241. On the right, the No. 2 Electric Turntable. There was also a clockwork track version.

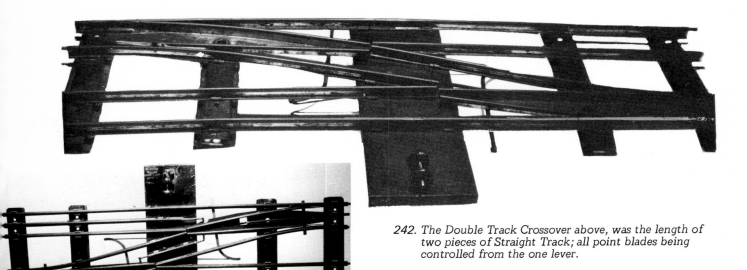

242. The Double Track Crossover above, was the length of two pieces of Straight Track; all point blades being controlled from the one lever.

242a. Overhead view.

243. Left, a Double Symmetrical Point. There were both 1 ft. and 2 ft. radius versions; the length of the branches being equal to a standard curved section of track.

244. The Point on the right is a Parallel Point with 2 ft. radius curved section. The branches fit to the Double Track section, clockwork in this instance. There was also one for electric rails.

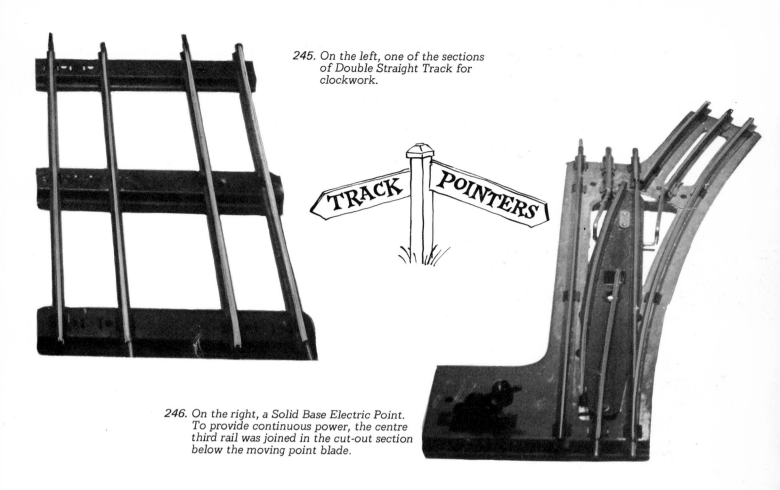

245. On the left, one of the sections of Double Straight Track for clockwork.

TRACK POINTERS

246. On the right, a Solid Base Electric Point. To provide continuous power, the centre third rail was joined in the cut-out section below the moving point blade.

247. Above, further examples of Hornby track. An Acute Crossing for 2ft. Curved Track. A similar piece for 1ft. Curves has longer arms. The centre Point is a 1ft. radius Point for Electric Track. The one on the right is a left-hand M.O. Point, not available with Electric Track.

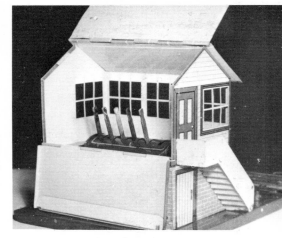

249. Signal Cabin with roof raised to show the levers in position.

248. The Control Point without the wire connected. It nevertheless illustrates the usefulness of this arrangement, as the adjacent Point has had the Point Lever removed to enable it to be used in a Double Track section.

CONTROL
SYSTEM

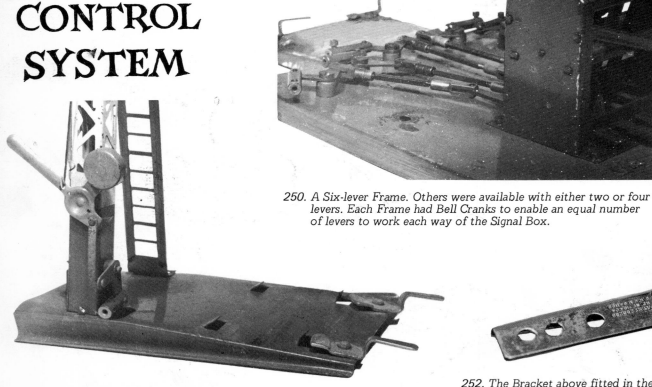

250. A Six-lever Frame. Others were available with either two or four levers. Each Frame had Bell Cranks to enable an equal number of levers to work each way of the Signal Box.

251. Above the linkage on the Signal Post and the clamps to secure the Signal to the track; thus preventing it moving when the lever was moved in the Cabin.

252. The Bracket above fitted in the U channel of the track sleeper, keeping the control wires in correct alignment parallel to the track. This part together with the other non-painted parts were all nickel-plated.

253. Left, an early No. 1 Buffer, designed for the early Hornby track with wire securing locks.

254. On the right, a Bing Buffer from a similar period and with a similar rail securing lock.

255. Another Bing Buffer. This hydraulic type is not as impressive as the Hornby version.

256. The No. IE Buffer Stop, which is similar to the No. 1, except for as the Hornby Catalogue put it "fitted for electric light". Seen alongside is the Lighting Accessory for fitting to the No. 2A and 3A Buffer Stops.

257. A late-comer to the range of Buffers, the No. 2A. It was 2/2d. cheaper than the No. 2.

258. Finally, on the left, are the 2E Hydraulic Stops, which tempted many a boy to run a Locomotive into them at full speed!

...END OF THE LINE

CONCLUSION...

Before the final page in this brief look along the Hornby Lines is complete, a view of the house owned by Frank Hornby at Maghull, Liverpool. The print was taken from a coloured photograph the original of which it is thought was taken by Frank Hornby, for he was very interested in photography as a hobby. However, his elder son Roland had a similar hobby and there is an opinion that Roland was the man who took the original negative. Despite the interest in photography in the Hornby household there are precious few prints of the hero of this book, hence the use of the Bronze on the frontispiece. This was made during the latter years of his life, possibly in 1930 or as late as 1935.

In assembling the facts for this little book it has been the pleasure and privilege of the writer to meet some of the people who knew and worked with Frank Hornby, and to listen whilst they retold with pleasure of the life and times they had in the company of Mr. and Mrs. Frank Hornby. Some have been recorded here, others remain a memory. Without the help of those mentioned here, all would have remained in diversity and the memory of Frank Hornby a little fainter.

Thankyou to Mr. and Mrs. W. Adams; Mrs. O. Gibbons; Mrs. M. Herbert; J. D. McHard, Esq. of MECCANO (1972) Ltd., Sir Peter Kirk, M.P., and the Staff of the House of Commons Library, Charles Gillett of the City of Liverpool Public Relations Office; Senator Fur Wirtscaft, Berlin; Bureau Federal de la Propriete Interectuelle, Bern; Prasident Des Deutschen Patentamts Munich; Gebr. Marklin and Cie GmbH.

Many of the photographs used were taken by the writer especially for this volume and are from the writers' own collection, but some owe their presence here to the generosity of the following members of the Hornby Railway Collectors Association; Mike Page (Cambridge) *plates 122 and 123;* Sr. Eduardo Lozano (Buenos Aires) for *plates 138 to 153,* and for much of the South American facts. Gratis Eduardo.

Also to the following members of the H.R.C.A. for allowing their models to be photographed by the writer; J. Gamble, *plate 193;* G. Horner, *plate 99;* Allan Daniels, *plates 167, 174, 175, 176;* Brian Dicker, *plates 46, 55, 116, 135, 137, 153a, 154 and 172;* J. Kitchen, *plate 105;* John Proctor, *plates 44, 106, 185, 186, 187, 188, 189, 192 and 195;* H. J. Swain, *plates 190 and 190a;* Ronald Truin, *plates 117, 181, 182, 183, 184.* Thank you Gentlemen, for your patience and your help. It is hoped that many of the favourite models of those childhood days have been presented here, some perhaps not seen before, some regrettably omitted.

Just some of the many toys made by Frank Hornby shown here, stand to pay silent tribute to the man whose belief in his ability to make a toy which would not be tired of too easily was justified, and as he had hoped, made his fortune. The toys, whether Meccano, Dinky Toys, the Hornby Series of trains, or the host of other minor construction toys gave a fortune of happiness to countless thousands of children. Thank you Frank Hornby.

HORNBY COMPLETE MODEL RAILWAYS

Complete Equipment for commencing the fascinating Model Railway Hobby

Hornby Complete Model Railway Sets provide the simplest way of beginning the thrilling Hornby Railway hobby. Four Sets are available and each is complete in itself; everything is there, ready for use as soon as you get it home

Unpack the box, then lay out the rails and accessories as shown in the illustration provided, put the locomotive and coaches or wagons on the track, and begin to run your own railway! It's the greatest fun in the world!

MECCANO LTD., BINNS ROAD, LIVERPOOL 13

THE RANGE OF HORNBY COMPLETE MODEL RAILWAYS

M8 Complete Model Railway
Consists of Locomotive (non-reversing) and Tender, Track, Goods Wagons, and other components for an attractive small home railway.   Packed in carton. Price **8/11**

M9 Complete Model Railway
The Locomotive and Tender are similar to those in the M8 Set. There are Passenger Coaches in place of the Goods Wagons, more Track and extra components.
Packed in carton. Price **11/6**

M10 Complete Model Railway
A larger Set, packed in a special cabinet. A fine range of components is included in addition to a Locomotive (non-reversing), Tender and Coaches   Price **18/9**

M11 Complete Model Railway
This is the best of the four Sets. It includes a fine reversing Tank Locomotive and all the accessories to make the splendid model railway illustrated below. The neat cabinet in which the Set is packed is shown in the reproduction herewith   Price **25/-**

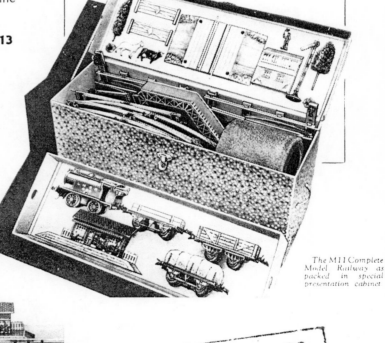

The M11 Complete Model Railway as packed in special presentation cabinet

How effectively the components of the M11 Complete Model Railway can be laid out is shewn in this illustration.